THE ILLUSTRATED NATURAL HISTORY

Scientific Consultants to the Series:

OF CANADA # The Arctic Coast DOUGLAS WILKINSON

Earth Science Consultant WALTER TOVELL, Director, Royal Ontario Museum. *Life Science Consultant* J. MURRAY SPEIRS, Department of Zoology, University of Toronto

Library of Congress Catalog Card Number: 76-109047
ISBN O-9196-4402-3
N.S.L. Natural Science of Canada Limited
58 Northline Road, Toronto 16, Ontario, Canada

Publisher: Jack McClelland
Managing Editor: Michael Worek
Art Director: Peter Moulding
Visual Editor: Bill Brooks

Editorial Consultant: Pierre Berton

THE ARCTIC COAST

Art Director: Peter Moulding
Artists: Vlasta van Kampen
Gordon McLean/Huntley Brown
Gus Fantuz/Jerry Kozoriz/Roy Irwin

Page 1: A solitary bull walrus.
Pages 2/3: Spear-fishing in the glow of the midnight sun near Pelly Bay.
Pages 4/5: Glacial majesty on Axel Heiberg Island.

Contents

THE ARCTIC COAST:

an album of maps   9

_____

PART ONE/**THE REGION**

1   The lowland Arctic   18

2   The mountain Arctic   22

3   The non-land of the
Arctic coast   26

_____

PICTURE STORY:

The Barren Grounds   31

_____

PART TWO/**GEOLOGY**

4   In the beginning   42

5   Birth of the
"Arctic" coast   47

6   The tundra biome –
the soil   52

_____

PICTURE STORY:

Native Man   57

_____

PART THREE/**PLANT LIFE**

7   The tundra biome –
the flora   68

8   Floral adaptation
to the cold   76

_____

PICTURE STORY:

The Living Arctic *79*

PART FOUR/**ANIMAL LIFE**

9 The air above *92*

10 Faunal adaptation
to the cold *101*

11 Invisible world of the
Arctic coast *111*

PART FIVE/**CONSERVATION**

12 Land of feast or famine *124*

13 Hunting man *132*

14 The destroyers *135*

Geologic time scale *143*

A short list of rocks,
plants and animals *144*

Bibliography *153*

Index *156*

Acknowledgements *160*

Prologue

The author in his kayak on the Arctic coast.

A WORLD FOR DREAMERS

The Arctic coast of Canada is a world for dreamers, a land few Canadians have ever seen or will ever see, a region about which we have come to know much but, as yet, understand little.

Natural history is a contemporary record of events that have occurred in the earth's past as seen through the probing, but biased, eye of literate man. Biased for many reasons; with few exceptions man is a creature of the mid-latitudes of earth. Throughout his long evolution he has lived in a world of regular rhythms—from the beginning of time he has watched the sun rise above the horizon in the east and set again in the west; night has followed day, followed by night again in endless sequence; season has followed season in uninterrupted pattern of cold and warm, or wet and dry. Beneath his feet man has usually felt soft soil supporting an abundant growth of grasses, flowers, trees, and an endless variety of mammalian life. Most important of all, in his mid-latitude world, man has always viewed the normal state of H_2O as liquid water and not as crystalline ice.

Can there then be any wonder that modern man is biased in his view of his Arctic regions—a land where the darkness of the cold winter night can last for two months or more, where the summer day can be a full five months long while the sun circles endlessly around the horizon to north and south each cloudless day, a land where ice and cold covering land, lake and sea is the normal condition for at least nine months of every year? Can there be any wonder that man has come to regard the cold climate of the Arctic coast as the sign of a disordered land, and the basic condition of cold as one of his greatest enemies?

Yet on the Arctic coast of Canada there are many areas where, during July and August, temperatures rise into the mid-sixties; where flowers bloom in clusters in the valleys and fields of Arctic cotton grass flutter and dance in the wind; where birds nest and insects buzz; where water is everywhere on the surface of the rolling land. But this brief period of summer warmth only serves to heighten the fact that, in the Arctic, winter is the main season of the year and the ice is never far away.

Yet in terms of extremes of cold, the Arctic coast must take second place to areas further south. The record low for the Arctic coast region is −63° Fahrenheit, a figure often equalled by points in northern Ontario and in the northern United States. The record low temperature for North America is −81.4° Fahrenheit, recorded in the sub-Arctic interior of the Yukon District, over 500 miles south of the Arctic coast. As well as not being the coldest place on earth the Arctic coast region doesn't have much snow; it is a desert area with a combined rain and snowfall averaging slightly under ten inches per year, about the same as that of the Sahara Desert in Africa. Although the winter snowfall in the Arctic piles into drifts that can be fifteen to twenty feet deep, the snow cover over most of the land amounts to only a few inches, a foot or so at best, per year. All winter long, on the windswept hilltops there is often no snow at all.

THE ARCTIC COAST:
AN ALBUM
OF MAPS

The full colour maps on the following pages of this album were especially commissioned for the series to illustrate the most important aspects of the natural history of the Arctic Coast region.

The photograph on the next two pages shows the area as seen from a satellite high above Greenland, facing westward.

Prudhoe Bay

Beaufort Sea

Herschel
Island

YUKON
TERRITORY

Cape
Bathurst

Aklavik •

Eskimo
Lakes
Franklin Bay

DISTRICT

Liard River

• Fort Nelson

BRITISH

ALBERTA

COLUMBIA

The top of the world

Four times, some geologists say five, glacial ice has crept out of the far north to inundate northern North America, Europe and much of Asia. Today we are still emerging from the last of these glacial assaults, the ice of which melted away from southern Ontario a mere ten thousand years ago, and which still covers sections of the Arctic coast region. Is the Arctic coast getting warmer or colder? Is the Arctic Ocean on the way to becoming free of ice, or will the ice begin to grow again to bury all the coast region under an icy mantle? Scientists are not sure and recent history provides only meagre clues. Pack ice issuing from the Arctic Ocean is dropping slightly in quantity; the southern limit of permafrost in Russia is slowly creeping north. But the Arctic coast is still a cold, cold land and will likely remain this way for some time to come.

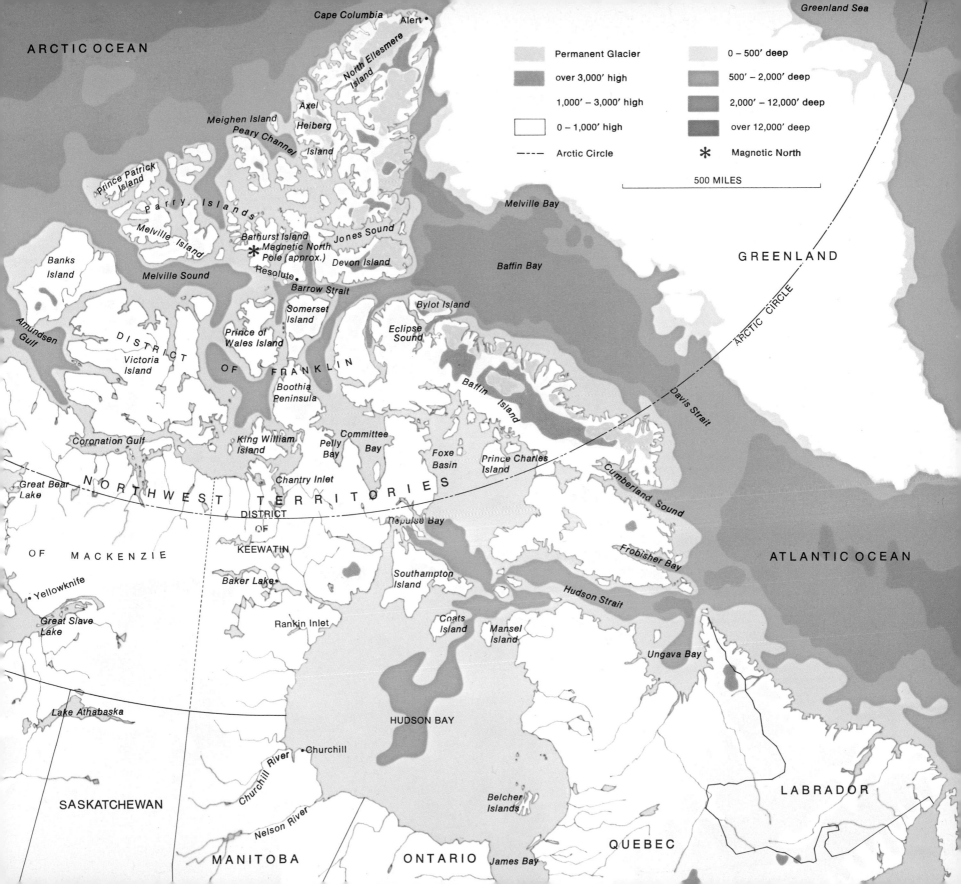

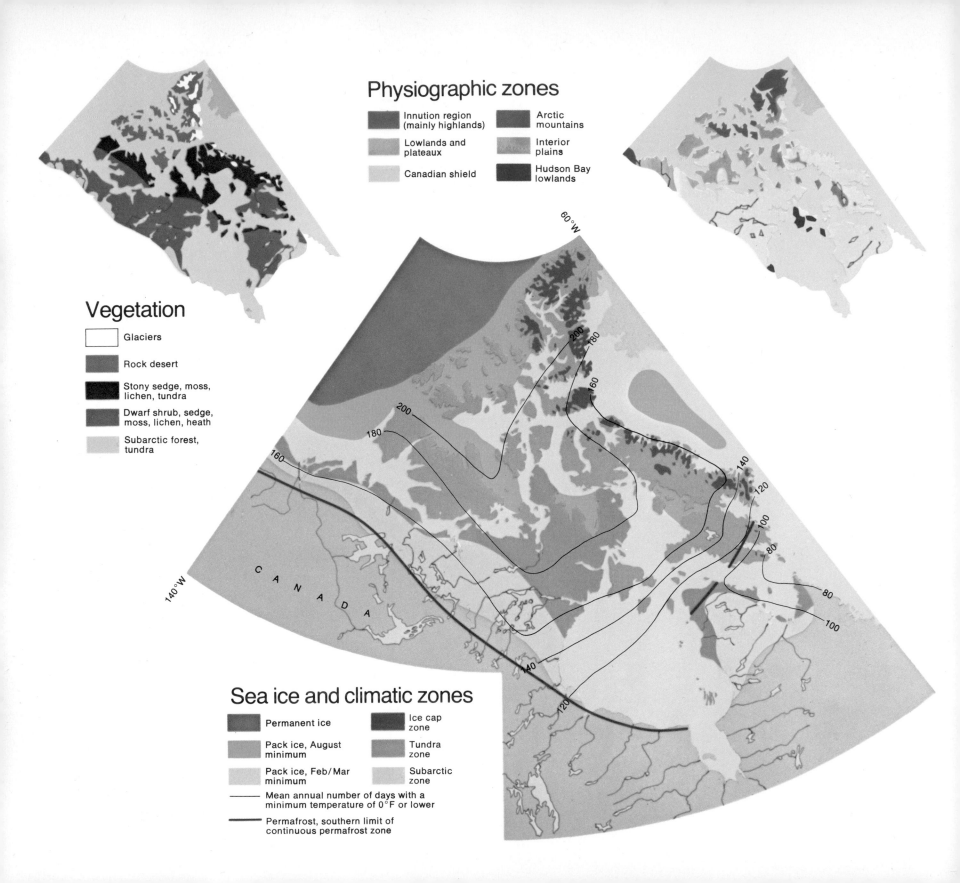

Physiographic zones

- Innuition region (mainly highlands)
- Lowlands and plateaux
- Canadian shield
- Arctic mountains
- Interior plains
- Hudson Bay lowlands

Vegetation

- Glaciers
- Rock desert
- Stony sedge, moss, lichen, tundra
- Dwarf shrub, sedge, moss, lichen, heath
- Subarctic forest, tundra

Sea ice and climatic zones

- Permanent ice
- Pack ice, August minimum
- Pack ice, Feb/Mar minimum
- Ice cap zone
- Tundra zone
- Subarctic zone
- Mean annual number of days with a minimum temperature of 0°F or lower
- Permafrost, southern limit of continuous permafrost zone

CANADA

60°W

140°W

200 180 160 140 120 100 80

Living and breeding in a far northern land

Note: In this illustration, the breeding ranges of birds are shown, along with the habitats of mammals.

Ringed seals are found everywhere along the Arctic coast, but rarely in open waters of big seas.

Rock ptarmigans live everywhere on the tundra and mountains, from lower Hudson Bay to Ellesmere Island.

Whistling swans are inhabitants of the lower Arctic in summer, but a few move far north to Baffin Island.

Polar Bears are found east to west, north to south; wherever there are ringed seals, there are polar bears.

Barren ground caribou, one of the very few mammals to migrate over great distances, live in open tundra.

Snowy owls are often seen in the south of Canada when food is scarce in their normal range of the north.

Red-throated loons, a summer only visitor, will nest as far north as there is land in the Arctic islands.

Musk ox are tundra dwellers found on many of the Arctic islands, and on the mainland at Thelon Sanctuary.

Arctic foxes live everywhere north of the tree line, on the treeless land in summer, wintering on the ice.

Gyrfalcons, during their white phase, can live in the Arctic all winter. Preys on birds and rodents.

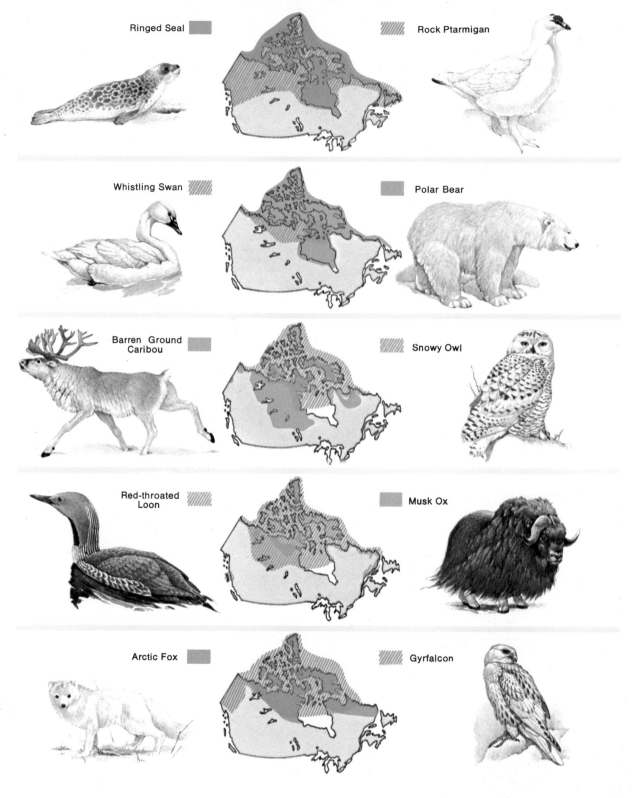

Ringed Seal

Rock Ptarmigan

Whistling Swan

Polar Bear

Barren Ground Caribou

Snowy Owl

Red-throated Loon

Musk Ox

Arctic Fox

Gyrfalcon

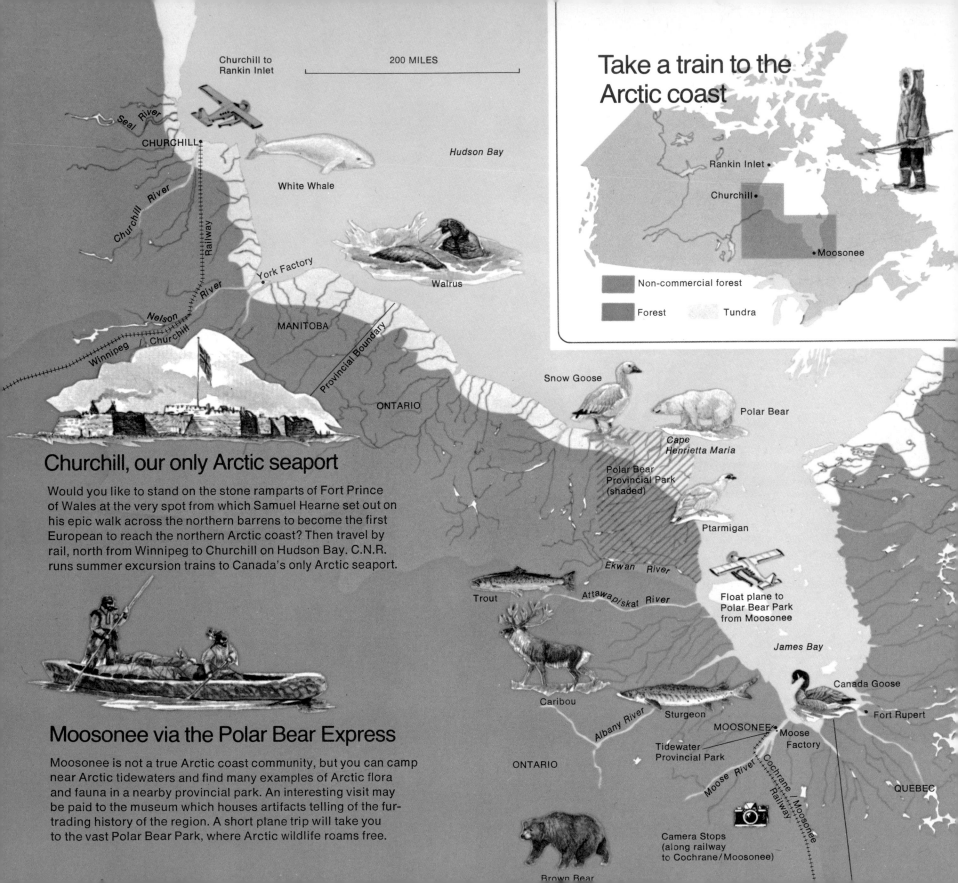

Take a train to the Arctic coast

Rankin Inlet •
Churchill •
• Moosonee

Non-commercial forest
Forest   Tundra

Churchill to Rankin Inlet

200 MILES

Seal River

CHURCHILL •

Churchill River

Railway

York Factory

Nelson River

Churchill

Winnipeg / Churchill

MANITOBA

Provincial Boundary

ONTARIO

Hudson Bay

White Whale

Walrus

Snow Goose

Polar Bear

Cape Henrietta Maria

Polar Bear Provincial Park (shaded)

Ptarmigan

Ekwan River

Attawapiskat River

Trout

Caribou

Float plane to Polar Bear Park from Moosonee

James Bay

Canada Goose

Fort Rupert

Albany River

Sturgeon

MOOSONEE •

Tidewater Provincial Park

Moose Factory

ONTARIO

Moose River

Cochrane / Moosonee Railway

QUEBEC

Camera Stops (along railway to Cochrane/Moosonee)

Brown Bear

Churchill, our only Arctic seaport

Would you like to stand on the stone ramparts of Fort Prince of Wales at the very spot from which Samuel Hearne set out on his epic walk across the northern barrens to become the first European to reach the northern Arctic coast? Then travel by rail, north from Winnipeg to Churchill on Hudson Bay. C.N.R. runs summer excursion trains to Canada's only Arctic seaport.

Moosonee via the Polar Bear Express

Moosonee is not a true Arctic coast community, but you can camp near Arctic tidewaters and find many examples of Arctic flora and fauna in a nearby provincial park. An interesting visit may be paid to the museum which houses artifacts telling of the fur-trading history of the region. A short plane trip will take you to the vast Polar Bear Park, where Arctic wildlife roams free.

PART ONE / THE REGION

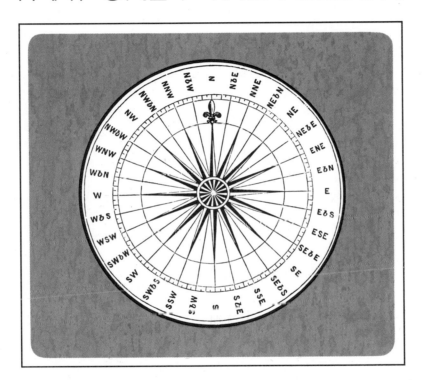

1 THE LOWLAND ARCTIC

Because it spreads across such a huge area of northern North America it will be apparent that the Arctic coast region is not one land, but several. In the northeast it is a land of high mountains, much of it covered by glacial ice. On the west coast of Hudson Bay it is a land so low that each incoming tide inundates miles of soggy mud and sand. On the north central coast it is a land of low rock hills; in the northwest it is a delta area; in the northwest islands it is a low, rolling land of mud and shale, and broken rock hills that, in very few places, rise more than a thousand feet above the level of the sea. Based on physiography the Arctic coast can be divided into a number of provinces. However, based on how it looks to the human eye and mind, the Arctic coast can be split into two main divisions—the lowlands, plains and plateaux Arctic; and the mountains and ice cap Arctic.

The lowland, plains and plateaux Arctic, hereafter called the lowland Arctic, makes up the bulk of the Arctic coast region – all the mainland Arctic coast, all the lower Arctic islands with the exception of the northeast coast of Baffin and Bylot Islands, all the central and western high Arctic islands, excluding only eastern Devon Island, Axel Heiberg Island and Ellesmere Island. Within this huge lowland area all land is generally less than two thousand feet above sea level; everywhere the horizon is gently rolling or flat, broken only by the occasional rocky headland or bluff. It is a horizontal landscape, its skyline unbroken by the sharp outline of high mountains, or by steep cliff faces rising up into the sky. Everywhere in the lowland Arctic there is a curious "sameness" to the landscape, brought about by three main factors: the smooth, rounded surfaces of the land as a result of scouring and/or deposition by massive glacial ice; the complete absence of trees or other vertical vegetation which would add variety in line, colour and perspective; the winter-long blanket of snow and ice that fills in the hollows of an already low, rounded landscape in a uniform white cover for most of the year. To these three factors can be added a fourth, one that affects all land areas on the Arctic coast—the absence of the works of modern man. On the Arctic coast there are no farms with their linear pattern of buildings and fences, no towns and cities with their vertical skylines, no systems of roads and railroads to pattern the land, almost no radio and television antennae, no power transmission lines to stand out against the sky.

In summer this lowland Arctic is a land of monotones with only the occasional splash of colour to relieve the generally brown or grey landscape—the white of Arctic cotton grass, the yellow of Arctic poppies, the mauve of purple saxifrage, the orange of lichens on the rocks, the yellow-green of moss in the valleys. Here and there along the edges of the sea are patches of green, lush grass to mark the sites of Eskimo camps of old where extra nitrogen has enriched the local soil. Great stretches of the lowland are bare rock, scraped clean and deeply grooved by glacial ice; other sectors are rugged hills of frost-shattered rock, generally dull brown or grey-blue in colour. Snaking across the landscape of the mainland Arctic west of Hudson Bay are the bright, bold outlines of sand and gravel eskers, materials deposited by sub-glacial streams during the waning days of the glacier lobes. Around the eskers hundreds of lakes fill every glacier-carved hollow in the rocky land; over fifty per cent of this area is under water in the summer. Everywhere the strand lines of former marine beaches rim the hills and the coasts with their low ridges of rounded stones and pebbles.

Underfoot the surface of the lowland Arctic presents one constant quality; it is almost all bad for walking. Pebbles, stones, boulders and sharp shale litter the surface of the ridges and the plateaux. The smooth, rounded stones of the raised beaches slip and roll underfoot. In the valleys the stream beds are a confused jumble of water-worn stones; the slopes dotted with close packed hummocks of frozen earth jutting up from swampy soil above the permafrost lid on the land. In many areas the tops of the rugged, rock hills are dotted with boulders of all sizes left behind by the retreat of the glacial ice. Everywhere, on swampy plain or rocky plateau, the lowland Arctic stretches out endlessly, flowing off to meet distant horizons, a vast empty land looking today much as it has looked for the past thousand years, as it will look far into the future.

In winter two new factors are added to the landscape of the lowland Arctic—snow and ice. Everywhere in the Arctic snow and ice must be considered as landforms for they will be the materials most underfoot during the greater portion of each year.

In the lowland Arctic snow and ice help to further smooth out an already horizontal landscape; the meagre snowfall sweeps clear of the hilltops and ridges to pile up in drifts in the hollows and valleys. In the rugged areas of bare rock hills the hilltops stand out against the white snow cover but in the plains country land, lake and sea blend into one surface of endless white. In the very flat lowlands of Foxe Basin or northeastern King William Island it is often necessary to dig down through the snow to find out if the surface beneath is land or sea ice. There is nothing to break the smooth curve of the distant horizon, nothing to distinguish a peninsula of land from the sea. In regions of great fluctuations in tidal flow, a rim of broken ice will mark the edge of the sea but, wherever the tide range is small, snow-covered land blends into snow-covered sea.

The snow that covers the Arctic lowland is dry and hard; only rarely does it fall free from the sky, usually it is whipped along by the winter winds, piling up into drifts, creating landscape in much the same manner as the wind-blown sand of the desert. Unlike grains of sand, snow granules pack tightly together in the extreme cold and, if allowed to come to rest in a hollow or in the lee of an obstruction, they quickly come to resist further attempts by the wind to remove them. Once formed, snowdrifts tend to remain in one place. However, the surface of the hard packed drifts can be eroded by the abrasive action of the hard snow granules of future blizzards; the upper surface of the drifts is carved into a myriad of delicately sculptured shapes and forms. In areas where the wind blows constantly from a single direction the resulting drift pattern on the snow surface will be an unending series of low, fluted ridges of hard-packed snow that run for miles across the tundra, a built-in winter compass for the overland traveller in this featureless land.

The hard-packed snow retains almost no indented footprint

The retreat of the glacial ice has exposed a mass of small stones over most of the lowland Arctic making walking difficult.

Once formed, snowdrifts tend to remain in one place, but the erosive action of hard snow granules can alter their shape.

to mark the path of man or beast. But it can retain an upraised mark of their passing. If a fox, or a bear, or a man walks over Arctic snow that has begun to pack but is not yet hard, the weight will press the snow under foot or paw more firmly in place than the snow all around. Wind blown granules of hard snow cut away the less firmly packed snow and leave a replica of the foot or paw raised in bold relief a few inches, often as much as a foot, above the level of the surrounding snow. This factor of snow compaction is used to advantage in the construction of Arctic airstrips and roads; snow is not ploughed as this would produce side hummocks and induce drifting; instead the snow is packed down by weighted rollers, if possible during the time when the wind is blowing hard. The wind then erodes the unpacked snow and leaves a road or runway of hard, compacted

snow that is raised above the level of the snow all around. The snow of future blizzards will blow right across it with a minimum of lateral drifting.

There are winter days in the lowland Arctic when the air is calm and clear, when the pale blue of the sky meets the gentle flow of the white horizon in a sharp line; when the only sound in the land is the sharp, rippling crack of the lake ice as it heaves and splits in the intense cold. Then the lowland Arctic is a vast, near-empty land of space, and peace. But there are far more days when the air is not calm and clear, when bitter winds howl down out of the northwest, carrying with them millions upon millions of tiny granules of hard Arctic snow, building into the infamous ground-drift of the Arctic tundra lands.

Ground-drift is a miles wide mass of whirling snow granules

Winds blowing at ten miles per hour or greater pick up snow from the ground and can reduce visibility to a few feet.

that can fill the air up to fifty feet above the surface of the land. Above the ground-drift the sky is often bright blue; from an aircraft flying at 5000 feet the snow-covered landscape below is clearly visible. But on the ground the whirling snow reduces visibility to as little as a few feet in every direction; the sun is merely an area of brightness in the whirling snow mass overhead. Arctic wind begins to pick up snow when it reaches a speed of about ten miles per hour, causing a light ground-drift condition. When the wind blows about twenty miles per hour the ground-drift will be moderate, horizontal visibility will be cut to a maximum of a quarter to half a mile. At thirty miles per hour the ground-drift will be severe, visibility generally less than one hundred feet; at forty miles per hour it will be difficult to see at all due to the effect of hard snow granules hitting the eyes.

Arctic ground-drift is often confused with white-out, another tundra phenomenon. Ground-drift is the result of blowing snow; white-out occurs in air free of snow particles, but under sky and surface conditions that cause a loss of depth of perception. White-out occurs most often when a low overcast of light clouds occurs above a uniformly snow-covered land surface, or sea ice surface, or glacial ice surface. Under such a condition the eye can see, but it cannot see anything; or if it can see objects, it is unable to see them in perspective. In a white-out it is not unusual for a person to walk right off a ten-foot high snowbank without ever seeing the drop, or to stumble over foot-high ridges of hard snow that cannot be seen. In a white-out there are no shadows, no relief, no perspective; sky and snow blend into one continuous, unending, all-encompassing entity. A foot diameter

21

rock on a small mound fifty feet away can be mistaken for a huge boulder on a high hilltop a mile away, and vice versa. A white-out condition can produce snow-blindness very quickly; with a bright sun the tendency is to shutter the eye to protect it but in a white-out the eye opens wide as it strains to see.

---

2 THE MOUNTAIN ARCTIC

In direct contrast to the horizontal landscape of the lowland Arctic is the terrain of the mountain and ice cap Arctic. This is the classic Arctic of mountain, snowfield, glacier and iceberg. Over much of the land areas of the eastern and far northeastern islands the landscape is vertical, and horizons are angular. Massive cliffs of red, brown and grey-blue rock rise sheer out of ice-clogged waters on the sea or loom silent and still against the blue-black, star-spangled sky of the long Arctic night. Coastlines in the mountain Arctic are indented by steep-sided fiords that twist and turn far into the land, often terminating in massive walls of glacial ice, the tips of long glacial tongues flowing down from the inland ice caps high above. Many of the Canadian Arctic coast fiords are immense; Admiralty Inlet cutting deep into north Baffin Island is the longest fiord in the world. It is very deep, just how deep is not known, but so deep that at one point about midway down the Inlet there is a huge patch of open water that remains ice free the year round, kept that way in the minus fifty below winter weather by the warm water welling up from the bottom far below.

In summer this mountain Arctic is often obscured by fog rising from the open water of the leads in the floating pack ice or drifting down from the icy slopes of the upper snowfields. Fog can cling to the mountainsides for days clamping a grey lid on the land, robbing it of most of its colour and vitality. But when the fog clears and the land and sea and ice stand out in bold relief, then the mountain Arctic coasts come to life. The white ice of the glaciers glistens and sparkles in the sun, each rock and snow cornice stands out hard against the blue of the sky. The colours of the rock—red, brown, grey-blue, sometimes yellow and orange where the lichens grow—glow with an intensity quite unusual in a land of monotones. The waters of the open sea reflect the blue of the sunny sky; on cloudy days the surface of the sea turns green. Every crevasse in every floating iceberg transmits pale blue or green as the bright sunlight shines through the ice, transforming it into opaque sheets of colour with only an upper surface of gleaming white.

In the mountain Arctic there is not usually the steady, strong wind that is so characteristic of the tundra. But cyclonic

A well-developed drumlin pattern is clearly distinguishable against the horizontal landscape of this section of southern Victoria Island.

winds from off the many ice caps can howl over the mountain valleys and far out over the sea ice with demonic fury. Such areas of high wind are very local, an important point to remember when travelling on the ground in a mountain Arctic region; no matter how bad the wind is, continue to move, for usually it will be only a short distance through to calm conditions again. But travel with caution for the extremely high winds off the glaciers and ice caps will blow dogs off their feet, if they get onto bare ice, to say nothing of the traveller himself. And if there is open water nearby be extra careful; a sudden gust of very strong wind and you could easily be blown bodily into the ice-cold sea.

In midwinter the Arctic coast region is a dim world, for long periods lighted only by the crisp white glow of moonlight reflected from millions of stars that twinkle and dance in the blue-black void above. In the far north there is no sunlight for weeks on end, in the far south it shines only for a few hours each day. Across the night skies of the Arctic coast, especially in the middle Arctic between latitudes 60° and 75° N. the ghostly light of the *aurora borealis* flickers and dances; the northern lights that have terrified and mystified peoples of the world since the earliest days of man. Today we know they are simply a neon-like glow induced in the upper air of the earth's atmosphere by streams of charged particles from eruptions on the surface of the distant sun, making the thin air glow in patterns of shifting,

weaving bands of light, sometimes coloured but usually clear white. Science tells us that no sound comes from these heavenly displays. But the words of the scientist fall on deaf ears of trapper and hunter of the far north, who, standing alone on a winter night, gazing upward in awe as the brilliant bands of cold fire weave their ghostly patterns across the vast, empty universe of space above, listen to the unearthly whispering of their faint message to the earth below.

In the far north regions of the Arctic coast it is late winter before light begins to return to the land. At first it comes as only a slight lightening of the southern sky about the hour of noon each day. Gradually the light period grows longer, and longer; the rays of the invisible sun, riding low beneath the horizon, send shafts of colour lancing across the pale blue and grey of the southern sky. For days on end sunrise is sunset, but each day it lasts a little longer, each day it gets a little brighter, each day the colours grow more vivid and intense. One day there is a brilliant corona of yellowish light on the horizon to the south, but it comes to nothing, and darkness falls again. It returns the next day, and the next, growing stronger until one day, at roughly the hour of noon, the huge, fiery red rim of the distant sun peeks above the hills to the south, rests there for a few minutes, and slips below the horizon. The sun has come back to the Arctic coast again.

As this time exposure shows, in summer the sun does not sink below the horizon but seems to merely circle the top of the world.

The White Glacier is retreating (left) and, as it does so, is slowly merging with the tongue of the advancing Thompson Glacier.

Everywhere the ice cliff is studded with embedded rocks, lined with many alternating layers of dark soil and white ice.

The noise at the cliff face can be deafening as huge blocks of ice tumble down to the ground.

A glacial trip to Axel Heiberg Island

Thousands of years ago immense masses of ice ground across most of Canada. Today only shattered remnants of the ice remain in the high mountains of the western cordillera and in the Arctic coast region. Most of the glaciers are in retreat, melting back slowly to return to the sea from whence they came long, long ago; but a few glacial tongues are advancing over the land, creeping down through mountain valleys, pushing huge masses of rock and soil ahead of them and carrying moraine materials and earth boulders within their mass. One such advancing glacier is the Thompson Glacier on central Axel Heiberg Island.

right: Scientist with ice drill on back pack scrambles over the surface of the White Glacier.

3 THE NON-LAND OF THE ARCTIC COAST

The thick ice cover on sea, lake and river is the non-land of the Arctic coast region. The ice is landlike; it is a major landform during most of the year, in many areas for all of it. Yet, each year the ice cover melts away, or it drifts away, or it drifts about, carried far and wide by wind and current, always to be replaced at its point of origin by other drifting ice, or by new ice that forms with the return of cold weather each autumn.

Men who have fought to get their ships through, or around, or over sea ice have invariably come to regard it as something very special in their lives. Like the Eskimo hunters before them, they soon came to realize that the simple term "sea ice" was wholly inadequate to describe a phenomenon of such complexity and power. Gradually they evolved a special vocabulary to describe sea ice in all its many shapes, actions and moods. Ice *makes* on the surface of the sea; in the early stages of its formation it is *slush* ice and *rind* ice, *pancake* ice and *young* ice. It becomes *one year old* ice, *two year old* ice, *three year old* ice; *winter* ice, *cake* ice, *brash* ice. On the surface of the sheltered inlets the smooth *sheets* of *land-fast* ice are *bay* ice. On the land-fast *floe* there is a *floe-edge*, an *ice-foot,* and *ice tongues*. On the open sea the *free-floating* ice is *pack* ice. *Fields* of *pack* ice are often hundreds of square miles in extent, made up of thousands of ice *chunks* that are *hummocked* and *rafted* into haphazard shapes and formations.

Sea ice can be *broken, weathered, cracked, submerged, rounded, honeycombed, rotten*. Floating with the sea ice are the massive *icebergs* and *ice islands* from which are *calved* smaller *growlers* and *bergy-bits*. Among the ice are *leads* of open water; on the ice surface in summer are *streams* of fresh water; amongst the Arctic Ocean *ice fields* are *polyanas* of open water. Into the air above the sea ice rises *steam-fog, sea-smoke, frost-smoke*; reflected in the sky is the *ice-blink* or *water-sky*. Within sea ice ships are often *trapped, nipped, crushed, heaved, elevated* and sometimes *buried*. This special language of the ice has grown so complex over the years that the World Meteorological Organization recently compiled and issued a basic list of standard English terms normally used to describe sea ice.

The freezing of the sea on the Arctic coast is a magnificent process. It can take place slowly, as is usual in the more southerly areas, or it can take place with startling rapidity as is often the case in the high Arctic. On north Baffin Island it is not unusual for an Eskimo to hunt over a sheltered bay by kayak one afternoon and then hunt on foot over the new ice of the same bay the following morning.

If the sea freezes over during a long spell of calm, clear cold, its surface will be as flat as a table top for miles in every direction, criss-crossed only by tiny, rounded pressure ridges caused by the expansion of the ice sheets in the deepening cold. But, if the wind blows hard during the early days of ice formation, then the smooth ice surface will be broken up into hundreds of smaller ice floes, each of which bobs up and down as it turns round and about on the heaving sea, rotating and rubbing one against the other, each tiny floe building up rough, raised edges of crumpled ice until the sea looks as if it is covered with hundreds of small, round griddles. This is the pancake ice of the sea. When the wind dies and the sea is calm again, these "pancakes" cement together into a new ice surface that is flat but not smooth, for now it is a matrix of hundreds of small pieces each with a raised edge cemented firmly to those of its neighbours. For a few days, or a few weeks, this new ice surface will form a patchwork of intricately interwoven tiny ice hummocks, until the next snowstorm piles the loose snow into drifts and cloaks the ridges beneath a hard white crust.

Sea ice can be land-fast, or it can be free-floating, or it can be a combination of both, split into two, sometimes three, sections by the action of the tide. Rimming the coast along the contour line of the highest tide is a narrow ice-foot that remains firmly cemented to the shore, building in thickness only at the times of the high tides. Out from the ice-foot, between the contours of the highest and the lowest tide, is a jumbled mass of broken ice and lumpy hummocks that is constantly being raised up and let down by the advance and retreat of the tide. Huge ice hummocks gradually build up over the many big boulders that lie on the bottom in the tidal zone, as the ever-thickening ice is repeatedly raised up and then lowered down onto the tops of the rocks. This area of rough, land-fast ice forms a new coastline in the winter, less visible in areas of low tidal range but spectacular in areas of high tides. On the coasts of Frobisher Bay, where the tide range is great and the waters are often shallow, an area of rough, broken ice in the tidal zone extends as much as a mile out from the rocky coast. Along the shores of the tiny enclosed harbour at the settlement of Repulse Bay, sections of the outer edges of the land-fast ice-foot terminate in sheer cliffs up to fifteen feet high whenever the tide is out. But the ice cliffs vanish completely when the tide comes in and raises the floating ice of the harbour up to the level of the ice-foot.

Beyond the rough ice of the tidal zone is the smoother ice of the land-fast floe, winter highway for the Arctic traveller on dog sled or skidoo. Floe ice covers the surface of all the inlets, sounds, straits and bays of the Arctic coast region. It grows out from the open seashores of Hudson Bay, Hudson Strait, Foxe Basin, Baffin Bay, Beaufort Sea and the Arctic Ocean, plus a few fast-water straits and sounds, to create enormous areas of new coast "land" each year. This land-fast floe ice extends out to sea for as little as five feet in areas with strong currents sweeping along deep water shores, or as much as five to ten miles in areas where the coast waters are shallow and quiet. Sometimes it is smooth and unbroken; sometimes it is rafted and hummocked. At the outer floe edge huge sheets of ice break off under the press of wind and tide to join with the main mass of the free-floating ice of the central pack.

The free-floating pack ice of the open sea is an enormous mass made up of hundreds of ice pieces ranging in size from huge, flat floes many hundreds of square yards in extent, to miles wide jungles of smashed and tumbled ice blocks that often send towers and pinnacles of tumbled blocks rearing thirty to fifty feet into the air. These huge areas of free-floating pack ice move about under the constant press of wind and current, some days separated from the land-fast floe by a wide stretch of open water, other days pressed hard against the floe edge by onshore winds so that along miles of land-fast ice edge, no open water can be seen. At times the ice of the central pack appears to be a silent, white desert stretching off to the horizon in all directions as far as the eye can see. But its mood can change in an instant; in moments it can shift, break up, thunder and charge about, ride up over itself, crush anything that lies in its path. The power of the sea ice moving under press of wind or ocean current can inspire only fear or awe; fear if you should happen to be helpless on a ship caught in its embrace, awe if you should be lucky

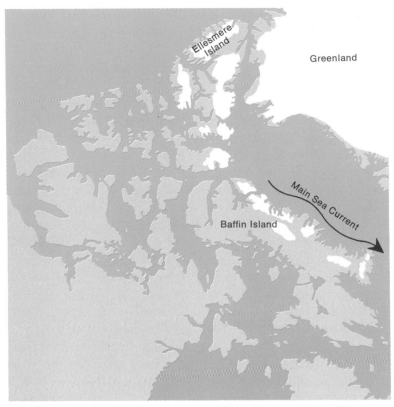

Arctic coast glaciers are shown in the white areas of this glacial map. Icebergs seen in the north Atlantic Ocean originate here.

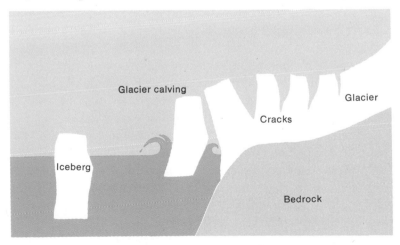

When the advancing glacier reaches the sea the massive weight of the ice breaks free and floats out to sea in the form of an iceberg.

27

enough to stand on a rocky shore and watch from the safety of the land as the charging ice turns a quiet strip of coast into a scene of wild disorder and din.

The ice that forms on the bogs and swamps, and on the lakes and rivers is the second form of non-land in the Arctic coast region; each year it converts great sectors of swamp and lake-dotted tundra into a continuous "land" mass across which animals and men can travel in any direction they wish. Although almost as important within the region as is the ice on the sea, freshwater ice has never been anything but ice to the men who have lived and travelled across the length and breadth of this far north land. For freshwater ice there is no stylized vocabulary, merely a few terms to indicate certain unusual conditions of the ice. Northerners hold ice on the sea in special regard; freshwater ice is merely taken for granted.

Late each summer on the Arctic coast the fresh water in the lakes and rivers begins to turn into ice. The surface layer exposed to the lowering temperatures of the air changes first, freezing into a thin, brittle film along the shores of all the ponds and streams, gradually creeping out to form an ever-thickening cover over the entire mass. Day after day, as the cold increases and the hours of daylight grow shorter, the ice grows thicker and thicker, clamping a tight lid on all the lakes and rivers in the land. If there is no snow and little wind the surface of the largest lakes freezes over flat and smooth as a marble table top, with ice so clear that fish swimming in the water far below are clearly visible from above. So transparent is this ice that it cannot be seen when looking straight down and one gets an impression of walking-on-water when travelling over the ice surface. Often this impression can lead to a mild panic developing as thoughts of plunging through the ice cover into the deep, cold water below begin to form in your mind.

Sometimes all during the late autumn, the outflow of water from the larger lakes will continue long after the river into which it flows has frozen completely, forcing the water to run over the top of the river ice, building up layer after layer of glistening new ice until the flow from the lake is finally stemmed. In a few localities the channels of large rivers are so confined that the turbulent, rushing water continually mixes the cold surface water with warmer water from below; such places remain free of ice all year round. Steam-fog rising above the tumbling waters of the great falls on the Kazan River, south of Baker Lake, can be seen for miles as it boils up into the forty below zero temperature of the midwinter air.

Many shallow lakes freeze to the bottom, as do the smaller streams and rivers. But the larger lakes do not; the amount of heat within the deep water layers is too great for even the intense cold of the Arctic coast to overcome. Ice on the major lakes reaches a maximum thickness of about six to eight feet sometime in March, early in the month in the southerly areas, later in the far north. Then follows a short period in which no new ice is formed while temperatures remain low but the returning sun brings warmth to the land. Heat from the sun affects the snow on the land first and melt water begins to run from the hilltops down onto the ice of the streams and rivers. The ice absorbs heat from the water and it too begins to melt; first in the smaller streams, then in the larger rivers, then on the ice of the lakes at the rivers' mouths, then along the shores of the lakes where the warmer, inflowing waters congregate. By mid-June in the south, somewhat later in the north, all the large lakes are free of ice around their shores but they still have a large free-floating ice cover in the centre.

Gradually this huge mass of centre ice melts. Shifted about by the wind it breaks up into smaller and smaller individual floes until it melts completely away, or until it is blown out of the lake into a river that will carry it off to the sea. Melting of the freshwater ice is a reversal of the process that formed the ice the previous fall. The ice absorbs heat from the air above and from the warmer water flowing under and around it; the millions of tiny air spaces within the mass warm up, particularly in the upper layers where the ice becomes honeycombed and disintegrates into a porous and jagged surface. The thick ice cover of the lakes, melted from above by the sun and from below by the warming waters grows thinner and thinner until it becomes a mere foot or two thick mass of ice crystals and entrapped pockets of air. This is the "candled" ice of the northern lakes, very dangerous to walk on for it crumbles to nothing beneath a person's weight. For days huge sheets of "candled" ice float about the larger lakes. Suddenly, almost as if by magic, the ice sheets disintegrate and disappear; the non-land surface of the lakes and rivers has become water again.

All along the mountainous northeast rim of the Arctic

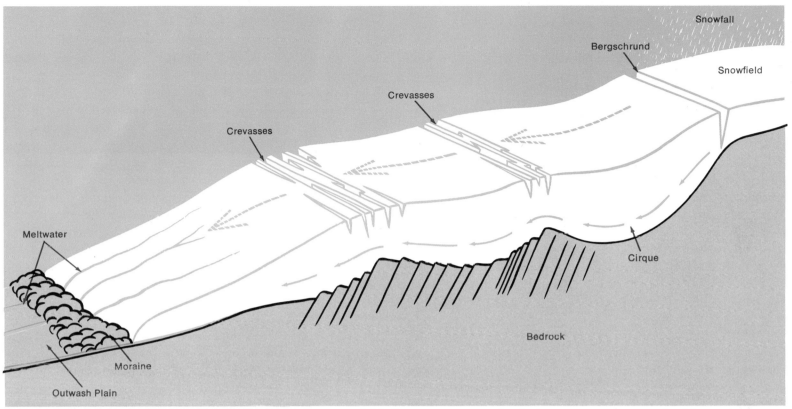

Crevasses

Snowfall

Bergschrund

Snowfield

Crevasses

Meltwater

Cirque

Bedrock

Moraine

Outwash Plain

A bergschrund is formed when a glacier pulls away from a snowfield. Crevasses open as the glacier passes over uneven land formations.

coast region is found the third form of non-land–the ice caps and glaciers of the Arctic islands. From Baffin Island in the south to Ellesmere Island in the far north much of the land is covered with ice in its most dramatic form; huge snowfields cover most of the highlands, spilling out through the mountain valleys into long, winding tongues of glacial ice, or spreading out in wide lobes across the upland plains and plateaux that slope down to the shores of the Arctic seas.

In the accumulation areas of the upper *snowfields* the snow and ice mass is *firm* or *névé*. At the outer edge of the upland snowfield there is often a large crack that develops where the ice begins to flow down over the steeper ground beneath; such a crack is a *bergschrund*. Glacial ice is said to be *plastic*; where it flows over steep drops or broken ground it bends and develops *crevasses* that cut deep into its surface. As it flows it picks up

debris–stones, rocks, boulders, gravel that tumble down onto it from the slopes above–to form *lateral moraines* along the edges. Two lateral moraines that meet on a piedmont glacier become a *medial* moraine. At the *terminus* of the glacial tongue the steep cliff of ice often pushes up an immense mass of rocks and boulders into a *push* moraine. Out from the terminus of the glacial tongue extends a wide *outwash plain* into which the swift, tempestuous streams of melt water cut and re-cut their tortuous channels. Water flowing out from the glacier is never clear; it is dirty brown wherever it flows out onto an outwash plain before heading off to the sea, and when it issues from the face of the glacial tongue directly into the sea or onto the steep bare rock floors of mountain valleys, the water is milky-white, heavily saturated with rock *flour,* the pulverized materials scraped from the land over which the glacial ice has flowed.

29

Wherever a glacial tongue flows from the coast to float on the surface of the sea it *calves* the immense chunks of ice called *icebergs* or *bergs* that are at last free to float wherever tide and current may take them before finally melting back to join with the waters of the sea from which they had come hundreds of years before.

The alpine snowfields and glaciers of the northeast Arctic islands provide some of the most beautiful and spectacular scenery in the world today. Near the centre of Axel Heiberg Island are two alpine glaciers, the White and the Thompson; the former is the smaller, draining out from a well defined accumulation basin of modest size. The Thompson is a huge glacier, flowing out from the immense McGill Ice Cap that covers almost half of Axel Heiberg Island. The White is a re-treating glacier, its gentle, sloping snout curves back to merge into the weathered and pitted surface of the long glacial tongue. At the end of the snout is a huge pile of unsorted rocks and small boulders that towers up as a terminal moraine over a wide out-wash plain.

Along one edge of its retreating terminus the White glacier merges with the mighty tongue of the Thompson; and the Thompson is a very different kettle of ice. It is an advancing glacier, its snout a fifty foot high, half-mile long cliff of jagged ice that towers up into the sky. In front of the advancing snout is an immense push moraine, nearly one mile deep, two miles wide and fifty to seventy-five feet high, a huge landform of gravel, stones and boulders complete with small lakes on its surface, that is being relentlessly pushed ahead by the steep face of the advancing ice. Everywhere the ice cliff is studded with imbedded stones and rocks, and lined with alternating layers of dark soil and white ice that are twisted and torn into wild swirls and tor-tured patterns; an artist's nightmare done in charcoal and chalk. From beneath the glacial snout a great stream of dirty brown water rushes through a narrow channel cut through the moraine, to dash headlong down an ever-shifting shallow cut that winds across the outwash plain to the sea.

The noise at the cliff face is deafening; the ice sighs and grunts as it shifts and settles; the crash of huge blocks tumbling down from the heights to shatter on the ice mounds below echoes across the wide valley. From a dozen openings in the cliff face great jets of milky white water shoot straight out, then curve majestically through the air to fall into the waters of the muddy stream below. Behind all is the noise of the main stream itself, a continuous, heavy thunder as the roaring waters hurtle along the shallow channel, rolling along the uneven bottom boulders of every size and shape that grind and scrape together in a never-ending deluge of sound and wild motion.

About half a mile back from the glacial front, where the ice of the Thompson first meets the ice of the White at the base of a high rock hill, is an enclosed, roughly triangular pocket formed between the walls of rock on one side and the walls of ice on the other two. Into this pocket melt water drains to build up a between-glaciers lake. Such lakes are common features in mountain glacier areas; they can be big enough to contain small icebergs calved from one of the glacial snouts along their shore, or small enough to be mere puddles. Between-Glacier Lake at the junction of the Thompson and the White is about a mile long and half a mile wide, large enough to have two small islands jut up from its surface.

Usually this lake drains off excess inflow each summer through a submarine channel to the outwash plain. But, in the summer of 1961 the weather over the entire high Arctic islands area was very warm; melt water in huge quantities ran into all the glacial lakes. Between-Glacier Lake level rose until the water overflowed and started to run over the ice surface of the White glacier in a wide, shallow wall of water nowhere more than a few inches deep. Swiftly, however, the running water began to cut a winding, twisting channel down through the ice of the glacial tongue; within hours the channel was twenty-five feet deep, within a day it was fifty feet deep and the waters of Between-Glacier Lake were draining out with tremendous force. The channel deepened until it cut right through the ice to the bedrock almost a hundred feet below. Along the bottom of this twisted, steep sided canyon in the ice a great torrent of muddy water smashed its way with enormous force as it raced pell-mell for the sea. At the terminus of the glacial tongue a wild river of water mixed with mud and rocks and boulders hurtled out through a deep slit cut through the terminal moraine. Within fifty-six hours Between-Glacier Lake was almost completely drained dry, and the long glacial tongue of the White was cut lengthwise by a hundred foot deep chasm at the bottom of which wild water still dashed headlong to the sea.

THE BARREN GROUNDS

Northern Boothia Peninsula is the furthest north part of the mainland of Canada. Largely uninhabited, even by Eskimo hunters, it is a bleak, near-barren peninsula, scoured by glacial ice, deeply incised by melt-water streams. In winter bitter winds sweep across its frozen surface, piling the meagre snowfall into huge drifts. Many drifts do not melt away in the summer but remain as visible evidence of just how massive glacial ice forms on a cold, northern land.

Elasmosaurid
(long-necked Plesiosaur)

Mosasaur

A warm beginning

Many millions of years ago much of North America, including most of the Arctic coast region, was inundated by the sea. In rocks laid down in the Silurian period there are unmistakable signs of coral reefs produced by warm water species that can exist only in seas constantly above 70°F. In rocks of the Cretaceous period that are now exposed on the west coast of Greenland (which was part of the north coast of North America at that time) there are fossils of such warm weather plants as breadfruit and fig. And the creatures of the deep, as can be seen here,

Hesperornis

Herring-like fish

Belemnites

were very different from those found in the icy waters of the Arctic region today. Far below the eerie glow cast by the dancing Northern Lights, giant marine lizards, mosasaurs, battled for survival against fearsome, forty-foot long reptiles known as plesiosaurs. Both of these marine animals were carnivorous, possessing sharp teeth, and used their strong paddles or flippers to propel themselves along. Other inhabitants of the warm Cretaceous seas were the hesperornis, a wingless diving bird that ate herring-like fish, and schools of belemnites, which resembled today's squid.

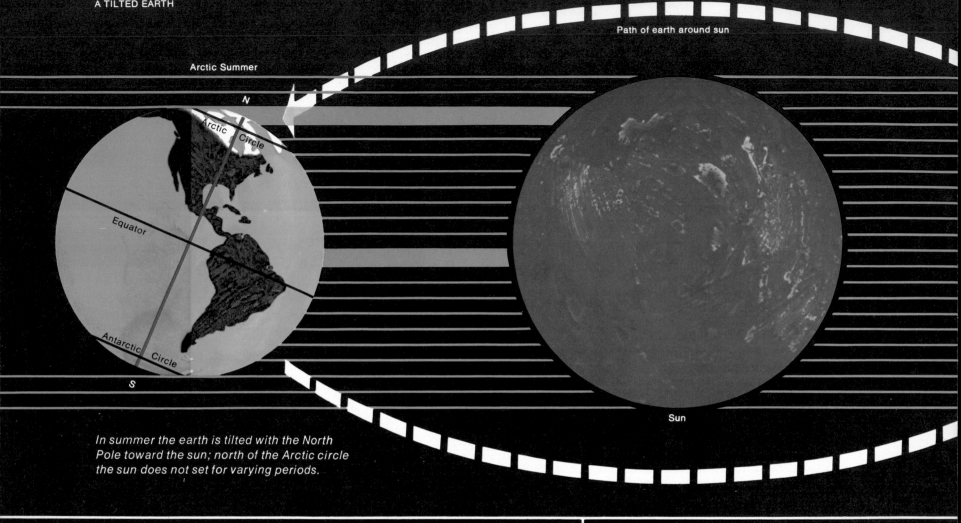

Path of earth around sun

Arctic Summer

N

Arctic Circle

Equator

Antarctic Circle

S

Sun

*In summer the earth is tilted with the North
Pole toward the sun; north of the Arctic circle
the sun does not set for varying periods.*

A gradual cooling

The weather on the Arctic coast of Canada isn't quite as cold as it is often
assumed to be; the extremes of low temperature in the world occur in the
interior of Antartica, in the deep, mountain valleys of the Yukon, and on the
vast wind-swept prairies of Russia. Nevertheless, the Arctic coast region
is cold, its basic weather governed by interaction of the four elements that
control all the weather of the world—the sun, source of radiant energy
that heats the earth and its atmosphere; the earth, because of its position,
its shape and the tilt of its axis in relation to the plane of its orbit about
the sun; the topography of the earth because of the way it guides, shapes
and obstructs the free flow of the air; and the atmosphere, a huge heat
engine driven by energy emitted from the sun.

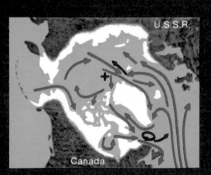

*Inflow of water comes from the north Pacific
(8%) and north Atlantic (85%). Outflow is
around both sides of Greenland.*

Arctic Winter

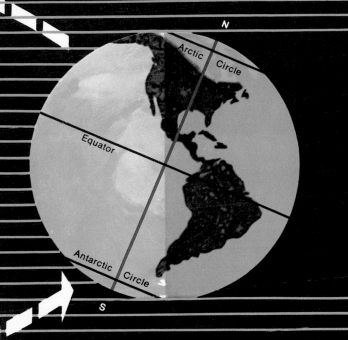

N

Arctic Circle

Equator

Antarctic Circle

S

In winter the tilt of the North Pole is away from the sun, and the Arctic coast, north of the Arctic circle, gets no light for days on end.

U.S.S.R.

Canada

Penetration of the Arctic by low pressure systems which cause cyclones occurs only in the far west and in Baffin Bay in the east.

ABSORPTION AND REFLECTION

Sea Ice

Sea ice melts from within due to salt concentration, and from the surface by heat convection from the air and meltwater. Over 60% of the thermal energy of the sun is absorbed by sea ice.

Snow

Soil and Rock

The bright snow surface on the land reflects over 80% of the thermal energy from the sun. This accounts in part for the much colder temperatures found inland than those experienced on the coast.

At one time the north pole of earth was in the vicinity of present day Hawaii, with the south pole in the south Atlantic Ocean. We know also that a great ice age occurred in the Permian period when almost all of Africa, India and also parts of Australia were under ice. Today, the south pole is in Antarctica which is completely covered by glacial ice, and the north pole is in the Arctic Ocean.

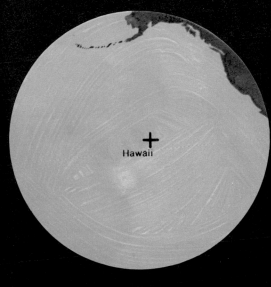

Hawaii

U.S.S.R.

Snow   Snow

Ice   Ice

Arctic Ocean

North Pole

Ice   Snow

Ice

Canada

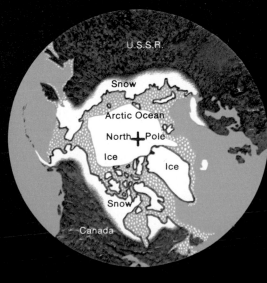

U.S.S.R.

Snow

Arctic Ocean

North Pole

Ice   Ice

Snow

Canada

Carved by the cold

The most spectacular form of ground ice is the pingo, ice-cored hills found in the Mackenzie Delta that are often a thousand feet high. Pingos are formed as a result of what is called a "closed" system of unfrozen soil developing within an area of permanently frozen ground. A large lake, beneath which there is no permafrost, fills with sediment or partially drains away (1). Permafrost will form on the bottom and sides so as to trap a huge core of unfrozen, water-saturated soil above it (2). Year by year, the freezing continues (3); hydrostatic pressure forces the water upward toward the surface of the land (4) to form a huge ice "pingo." Polygon soil formations pattern great areas of the Arctic. The ground cracks during freezing in the autumn, water collects in the cracks where it freezes to form tapering wedges which continue to grow and fracture year after year, driving the soil into saucer-like depressions of polygon shape.

THE FORMATION OF A PINGO

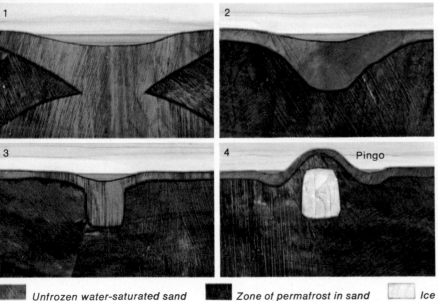

1
2
3
4   Pingo

Unfrozen water-saturated sand   Zone of permafrost in sand   Ice

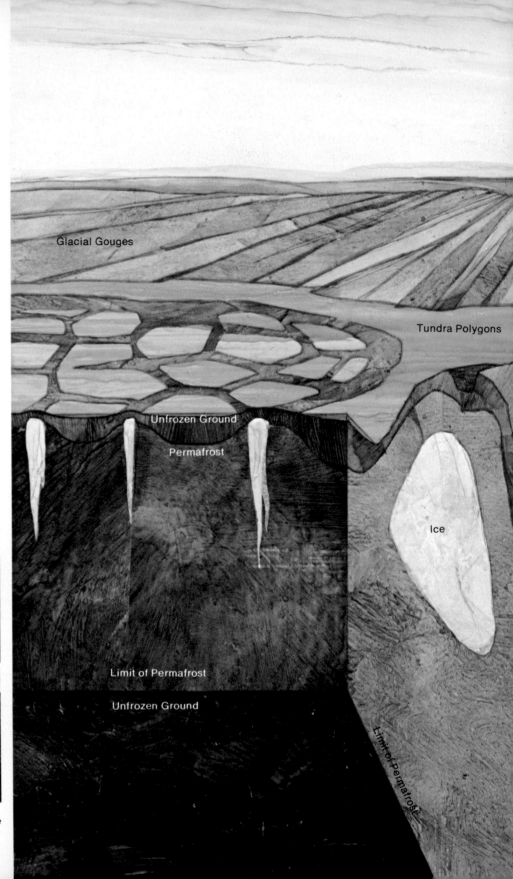

Glacial Gouges

Tundra Polygons

Unfrozen Ground

Permafrost

Ice

Limit of Permafrost

Unfrozen Ground

Limit of Permafrost

Pingo

"Drunken" Forest

Stone Rings

Ice

Unfrozen Ground

Permafrost

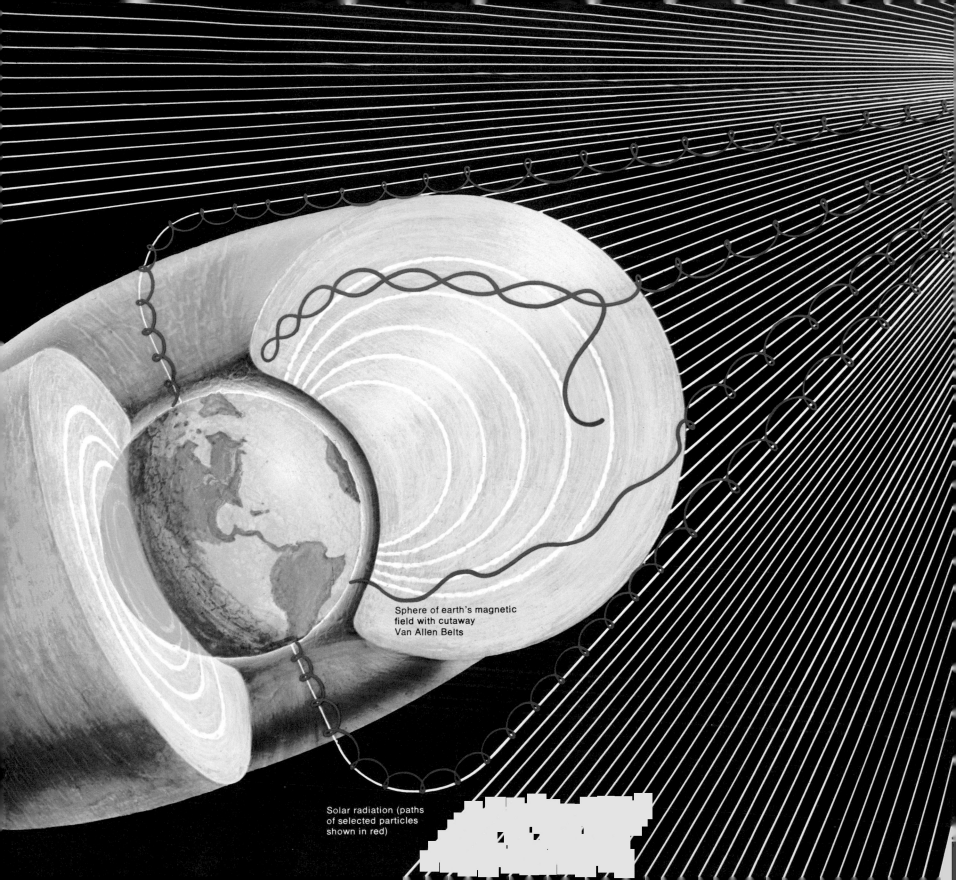

Sphere of earth's magnetic
field with cutaway
Van Allen Belts

Solar radiation (paths
of selected particles
shown in red)

Solar flare

Aurora borealis – strange illuminations in the night

Displays of Northern Lights, *aurora borealis,* generally occur at the southern sector of the Arctic coast sky. High above the earth are the Van Allen Belts, two great bands of radiation materials trapped in the earth's magnetic field, which trap, in turn, most of the deadly radiation material emitted by the sun, thus protecting all life on earth from this lethal solar rain. But the Van Allen Belts are shaped like a doughnut, with the hole over both north and south polar regions. Thus protection from solar radiation is very slim on the Arctic coast of Canada, so slim that airliners flying the polar routes during times of maximum emissions from the sun must fly at substantially lower altitudes in order to minimize possible hazard to passengers on the planes.

Electrically-charged particles from a solar disturbance (left) bombard the outer Van Allen Belt, causing a magnetic storm which can black out high-frequency radio communications. The most spectacular visible results of this upper atmosphere impact are auroras, and in the north the display is known as the aurora borealis.

The airplane (right) is flying within the troposhere, the lowest level of a complex, many-layered atmosphere, and the one in which man exists. This level ends at 5 to 10 miles above the earth and contains the air currents which shape most of our weather. Glimmering displays of light hang like curtains at the upper levels.

MILES

600

500

400

300

200

100

The mountains of Baffin Island.

PART TWO / GEOLOGY

4 IN THE BEGINNING

5,000 million years ago there was no Arctic coast region of Canada; there was only the proto-earth, gradually cooling, gradually shrinking, gradually forming a thin crust over its mantle of warm, viscous rock.

About 4,000 million years ago rock flows from within began to build what are now the shield areas of the earth. The shields were formed originally by the deposition near the surface of masses of light, granitic rocks carried up from deep within the mantle by convection currents in the viscous rock. These masses of lighter rock gathered together in the eddies formed between the huge, slow-moving currents, at the point where the currents met near the surface and deflected downward as they cooled and sank. As the lighter rock gathered in the eddies it began to build up; the masses grew thicker and wider through the constant addition of new materials on the bottom and the sides. Eventually they broke through the surface crust to rise as mountains, high above the shallow seas. The bases of these shield mountains floated deep in the heavier basaltic rock of the mantle similar to the way in which the base of an iceberg floats deep in the supporting sea. Like the iceberg, the bulk of the shield mountain mass lay beneath the surface of the earth. Today, with the tops of the mountains worn away, the deep roots remain, and the crust of the earth is much thicker under the continents than it is under the surrounding seas.

The shields are the ancient nuclei of the present continents. There are nine such areas in the world and the largest single mass is that of the great Canadian shield which forms the geologic base for over half of Canada, and for over three-quarters of the Arctic coast region. This Canadian shield represents the most stable area of our land surface, but this was not always so. During the long Precambrian era, the Canadian shield was the centre for a number of great revolutions of the earth's surface, each involving the building of high mountains. But, from the moment the rocks of the shield mountain rose into the atmosphere they were subject to all the forces of erosion. They began to wear down and the material of which they were built was carried as sediment to be deposited on the edges of the shield.

Over long periods of geologic time these sediments were compressed into sedimentary rocks and many areas of such rocks were themselves raised up into new mountains by forces acting from within the earth. Sedimentary rocks were often changed into metamorphic rocks through intense pressure and heat when they were buried deep in the earth because of subsidence of the land and then brought to the surface again when the land of which they were a part rose again into the sky. The same forces behind these movements brought to the surface new rock materials, magma, and forced it through the earth's crust with extreme violence, in the case of volcanoes, or with slow, majestic movements in the case of immense lava flows issuing from fissures. On the surface this magma cooled to become igneous rock, to form new mountains which the forces of erosion began to attack immediately and slowly wear down.

This complex, slow process of change and mixture in the rocks of the Canadian shield went on through millions of years of time – more than five-sixths of the total time span since the earth was formed. The older rocks are in the shield core, the younger toward the outer edges, showing that the continent has grown laterally through geologic time, spreading out to form the land area now known as North America. Millions of years of erosion and deposition of materials transformed the original shield mountains into a great plenaplain, much larger in area than the original shield but nowhere very far above sea level. The profile of this great plain was that of a large dome, sloping gradually down from the centre to lower outer edges on which rings of deposited materials had built up, prior to being raised high into new mountain ranges. In the far north, most of the present Arctic archipelago formed the outer edge of this great continental plain and the north coast extended much farther east, north and west than it does today. The present site of Hudson Bay was land. There was, in effect, no Arctic coast region as we know it today; throughout most of the four and a half billion years of earth history the changing geology of what is now the Arctic coast was similar to that of the remainder of the Canadian shield. The sequence of geologic events in the northern sector produced results that were similar to those in the rest of the shield to the south.

The relief outline of Canada today is that of a great trough having a general northwest-southeast axis. On the west side of

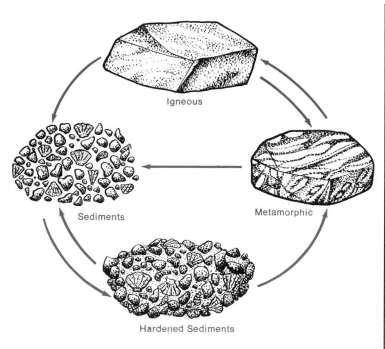

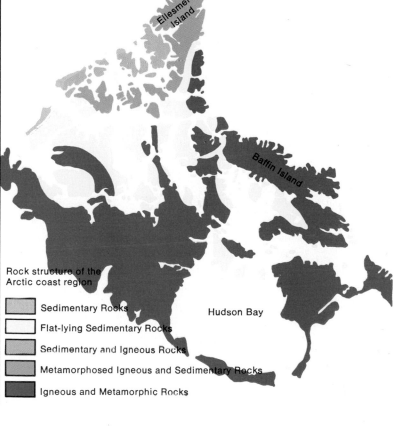

Rock structure of the
Arctic coast region

Sedimentary Rocks

Flat-lying Sedimentary Rocks

Sedimentary and Igneous Rocks

Metamorphosed Igneous and Sedimentary Rocks

Igneous and Metamorphic Rocks

The basic elements of the earth's surface can be combined into many forms. Hard igneous rock exposed to erosion disintegrates into sediment, is later compressed by pressure within the earth into solid sedimentary rock and the process starts again.

the trough the land rises up into a continuous series of mountain ranges that run the length of the Yukon and British Columbia; on the east side are the mountains of the northeast Arctic islands, Baffin Island and Labrador. In between the east and west mountains is the main land mass of Canada; a region of lowlands and uplands, plains and plateaux. The Arctic coast region consists of the northeastern third of this huge trough; along the east side are the high mountain ranges of Ellesmere, Axel Heiberg, Devon and north Baffin Island, and the lower mountains of south Baffin Island and the northern tip of Labrador. From this mountainous region the land slopes down to the southwest through uplands and plateaux to plains and lowlands in the central areas. In the west it rises again to plateaux that are 3,500 feet above sea level, but drops off again to a low coastal plain in the extreme northwest. Down the centre line of the

trough, the low area is not continuous but is made up of a number of basins separated by higher ground, or divided one from the other by tongues of upland. In general, the physiography of each basin is related to that of all the other basins, an indication that the entire Arctic archipelago was, at one time, a continuous land mass, parts of which are now submerged beneath the sea.

The basic structure of the Arctic coast region consists of two types of rock. By far the greater part is underlain by Precambrian rocks of the shield that lie like a huge, irregularly-shaped doughnut under the central and eastern portions of Canada, with the water mass of Hudson Bay as the hole in the centre of the doughnut. In the Arctic coast area all of Ungava, all of Baffin Island except for the northwest corner and a small piece of the west coast, all of the Keewatin District on the west coast of Hudson Bay, most of the Arctic sector of the District of Mackenzie, and small segments of the western islands are underlain by the rocks of the shield.

Upon these ancient rocks, worn down by erosion through the tremendously long passage of most of geologic time, have been deposited sedimentary rocks ranging in age from Palaeozoic to Tertiary. These sedimentary rocks form a wide belt through the central and western Arctic islands from the north coast of the Mackenzie and Yukon Districts through Victoria, Banks, King William, Prince of Wales and Somerset Islands, and on into Devon and southern Ellesmere Island in the high Arctic. Portions of the outer edges of the western islands of the high Arctic are also of sedimentary rock, as are sections of the many northern peninsulas of the mainland west of Hudson Bay, parts of all the islands in Hudson Bay and Foxe Basin, and the northwestern corner of Baffin Island. Most of the high Arctic islands area is underlain by moderately folded rocks ranging in age from Precambrian to Cretaceous. At one time there must have been a fairly deep and uniform cover of these sedimentary rocks over the Precambrian rocks of the shield in all sectors of the Arctic coast region. But most of this cover was removed by the scouring action of the glacial ice during the successive flows of ice across northern North America during the million years of the Pleistocene period, leaving great areas of the Arctic coast almost denuded of its sedimentary rock cover and obliterating the record of much of its early history. It is interesting to speculate that much of the fertile soil now covering various parts of southern Canada was originally sedimentary rock in the Arctic, transported to present localities by the movement of glacial ice.

There is a lack of detailed information on the early geological history of the Arctic coast region, partly due to removal of the record of the rocks by the glacial ice and partly due to a lack of study brought about by problems of travel to and within the region that were not solved until very recent times. Geologically the region can be broken down into areas that are closely related to other regions of Canada: the Arctic coasts of Hudson Bay form part of the northern half of the Canadian shield; the central Arctic and the western Arctic islands area is an extension of the Plains region to the south; the high mountains of Baffin, Devon and southern Ellesmere Islands are edge-of-shield mountains, similar in formation to the mountains of the Cordillera region of the west; the low mountains of southern Baffin Island and Labrador are similar to the Appalachians.

Because of this wide variety of topography the Arctic coast region cannot be said to be a cohesive unit by virtue of its geology; rather it is a region due solely to its uniformly severe, cold climate. However, there is a good deal of evidence to show that the area now occupied by the Arctic coasts of Canada has not always had a cold "Arctic" climate, that it has been related to other parts of Canada not only geologically but in climate, flora and fauna as well. Until the late Tertiary period the entire Arctic coast region was the northern extension of a continental land mass, with a climate to match that of southern Canada, varying from temperate to sub-tropical most of the time. The sequence of events that produced the surface contours and present climate, flora and fauna of the Arctic coast, in effect creating the Arctic coast region, did not begin until well into the Tertiary period, most likely about twenty million years ago, when there occurred the uplift of the eastern and northeastern mountains from Labrador to Ellesmere Island and the concurrent depressing of the land to form the deep basin of Davis Strait and Baffin Bay. At about the same time a new period of mountain-building broke out in western Canada along the length of the Cordillera, and the entire Arctic coast region, along with almost all of northern North America, rose until it stood about three to four thousand feet higher above sea level than it does today.

The combined factors of the great uplift of mountains in the northeast and west, and of the higher general elevation of all the land of northern North America, were to be of tremendous significance in the next stage of the natural history of the earth, and for the Arctic coast region in particular. For it was following this period of mountain-building and general uplift of the land that the world's most recent ice age settled in over the northern lands of the world. Until this time there had been no "Arctic" coast region. It wasn't until the beginning of the Pleistocene period, about one million years ago, that the natural history of the cold "Arctic" coast region of Canada really began.

In the tidal zone ice lying over boulders on the sea floor is cracked and forced upward with each falling tide. By late winter jumbled ice hummocks over this boulder may be fifteen feet high.

5 THE BIRTH OF THE "ARCTIC" COAST

Accounts of the glacial age in North America during the Pleistocene period usually begin "About a million years ago the climate over the northern hemisphere grew colder. . . . " While this statement is true, it is somewhat misleading, for there is no way of knowing at present if the temperature fell and the climate grew colder so as to initiate conditions that led to the formation of glacial ice. Certainly the climate over the northern hemisphere grew colder once the basic element or elements required to set in motion an ice age came about. But the actual condition or conditions required to start an ice age are speculative, and a lowering of the earth's temperature may or may not have been one of them, as is shown by the theory of a warming climate precipitating the ice age of the Pleistocene.

It is known that about one million years ago, for reasons not yet clearly understood, the universal warmth which had bathed the earth for the 200 million odd years of the Mesozoic and Cenozoic eras gave way to a time of fluctuating temperatures in the northern hemisphere. Gradually, over many thousands of years, the seasonal fluctuations increased and the period of cold grew longer each year. The cold winter rain changed to snow which melted away each summer. As the years flowed on, as the centuries passed one into the other, the time of melting was delayed a little later each year, the time of the first snowfall arrived a little earlier. There came a summer when a few patches of winter snow did not melt but remained on the ground to be buried by the new snow of the following winter. On the Arctic coast this most likely occurred first in the high mountain areas of the far northeast, and only a little later in the lower mountains of the southwest.

Winter followed winter, each a little longer, each piling up new drifts of unmelted snow throughout the Arctic coast region until the mountains of the east and west and all the far north land areas were buried year round under unmelted snowdrifts with only the steep faces of the mountain peaks clear of snow.

"Candled" freshwater ice in the final stage of summer melt – the thawing ice settles into hexagon pencil-shaped crystals as it melts.

The snow didn't fall evenly, some areas received more than others, areas that were in the proper geographic location for heavy snow to fall almost continuously and build up many times faster than elsewhere. As the centuries passed the snow in these areas of extreme accumulation became thicker and thicker—tens of feet, then hundreds of feet. Weight compacted the snow into ice, as a ball of snow is compacted into ice by squeezing it in the hand. Deep down in the ever-thickening ice masses the pressures were enormous, so great that the seemingly solid ice began to act in a strange way—it began to flow out in all directions, guided only by the contour of the land beneath or about. Slowly but relentlessly the ice pushed out from its source areas, propelled by the continuing pressure of the new layers forming at the centre of the mass.

In the mountains of the northeast the ice flowed along the valleys, or it carved out new valleys in the softer rock, or it built up to over-ride the mountain ridges. On the plateaux and plains it oozed over the land in all directions, pushing out immense, bulging lobes of glistening white. The fronts of the lobes, and of the glacial tongues in the valleys, were huge cliffs of jagged ice that ground across the land surface like the blades of enormous bulldozers, scraping up the loose soil, grinding the sedimentary rock cover of the land into a mixture of silt, sand, pebbles and boulders, pushing it ahead with irresistible force or plastering it onto the land in layers of sticky clay. This grinding and stripping of the softer rock was aided by a matrix of rock particles in the bottom of the ice mass; the bottom of the glaciers were rock-studded grinding tools with undersurfaces not unlike pieces of giant emery paper. The embedded rocks did not stay in one place but were constantly being rolled about in the bottom of the ice as it ground over the land, presenting fresh edges to gouge the land beneath.

Over thousands of years the ice kept accumulating and spreading out over the land. By the time it stopped, a huge mass of glacial ice buried all of Canada, except for mountain peaks in the Cordillera and northeast Arctic islands, some pockets in the Yukon Territory and the outer fringe of western Arctic islands. The ice was thousands of feet thick, about three miles deep over the present site of Hudson Bay. The vast amount of water locked up in the ice caps of the northern hemisphere lowered the level of the earth's oceans between 300 and 400

Caribou

Musk Ox

Alaska Brown Bear

Grey Wolf

Red Fox

Arctic Fox

Wolverine

Ermine

In Pleistocene times the massive accumulation of water in the glacier ice caused a lowering of the sea level, permitting a few hardy animals to cross the Bering Strait from Asia to America.

feet, exposing nearly two and a half million square miles of new coastal land. Because of this North America was connected to Asia by a land bridge across what is now Bering Strait.

Then, either the temperature grew too warm for the snows of winter to remain on the ice divides the year round, or the source of the water supply vanished, or a combination of both occurred. Without new ice to push out from the source areas, the glacial lobes and tongues began to thin down and to melt back from their leading edges. Once started, the ice melted back quite rapidly, much faster than it had crept down across the land. It didn't melt evenly, or at a uniform rate; sometimes the melt was rapid, then it would slow down for a while. It might even make small local advances. But, over a few thousand years, all the great mass of the ice sheets melted away.

For many thousands of years Canada, its far north included, remained largely free of ice with a climate not unlike the one it has today. Then, the ice began to form again in the accumulation areas, and to flow out over the land. Before it stopped all of Canada and much of the northern United States lay buried beneath glacial ice once more. This time the ice advanced even farther south, reaching to within 650 miles of the Gulf of Mexico in the central U.S.A. It remained for a longer period before melting almost completely away. Four times, some say five, the glacial ice crept out of the north and west this way and retreated back again; each time the ice advance lasted for about 100,000 years while the intervening warmer periods when the land was ice free were much longer, the longest about 300,000 years. Today we are living in the last stage of the latest retreat of the ice and no one is sure that it will not start south again.

One of the most intriguing questions about the ice ages of the Pleistocene, and about ice ages in general, is what caused the ice to fluctuate, to flow out and then pull back so many times, and possibly will cause it to flow out again in the future. An interesting, and quite plausible explanation, that seems to fit the facts of the glacial advances and retreats as they are known to have happened in Canada, and one that has some direct evidence found in bottom deposits laid down in the north Atlantic Ocean during the Pleistocene to support it, hinges around a rather startling possibility—that of an open polar sea.

It must be remembered that two main elements are vitally necessary before snow can fall and accumulate on the ground in sufficient quantities to produce masses of glacial ice—very cold temperatures over large areas for a major portion of the year, and a huge source of water nearby, lying in the direction from which the prevailing winds blow. Without sufficient water cold alone cannot produce glacial ice, which is why much of Alaska in the far northwest escaped being covered with ice during the Pleistocene ice age even though it must have had a very cold climate.

There is evidence to suggest that the Arctic Ocean was free of ice at times during the Pleistocene period. If so, the normal flow of air in the northern hemisphere would have brought polar winds down across a long stretch of ice-free Arctic Ocean, picking up moisture as they flowed south and warmed up. These moisture-laden winds would have blown across the north coast and up the slope of the northern mainland, which at the time of the late Tertiary and early Pleistocene was an upland about 3,000 to 4,000 feet higher than it is today. The winds would have dropped their moisture as they rose over the land, and in the deep interior of the continent this moisture would have fallen as snow at the higher altitudes. The winds would have caused tremendous blizzards in the interior of northern Canada.

A similar situation would have applied to winds blowing off the north Atlantic Ocean onto the high land of Labrador and northern Quebec; winds from off the north Atlantic Ocean, the Greenland Sea, Baffin Bay and Davis Strait would have dropped snow on the mountain areas of Greenland, Baffin Island and the eastern high Arctic islands. And it is quite probable that, long before this happened, there were already permanent snowfields in the very high mountains of the western Cordillera region of British Columbia and the Yukon.

Once the ice caps had developed and risen to heights of thousands of feet in the accumulation areas and had flowed out to merge together, the massive ice mass would have become a major landform that would further reinforce the intensive accumulations of snow and its conversion into glacial ice. The blizzards produced over the accumulation areas must have been of an intensity and degree of violence as is found only in the Antarctic continent today. In the area of what is now Hudson Bay they must have been especially fierce, with winds from the north Atlantic storms meeting and battling with the winds from off the Arctic Ocean. Small wonder that this area is thought to

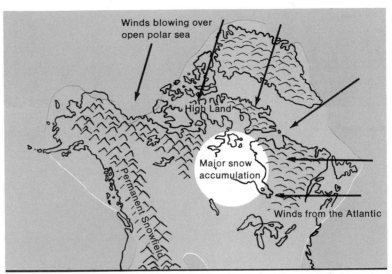

During the Pleistocene cold winds blowing over the open sea picked up moisture, which later fell in the form of snow when the air masses rose to traverse the uplands. The area around Hudson Bay, became the centre of major snow accumulation.

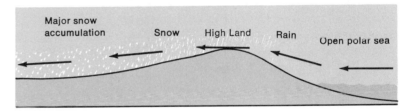

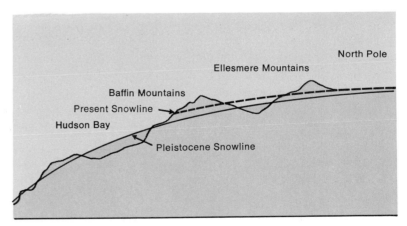

A moderate lowering of the snow line placed large areas of the plateau in the zone of snow accumulation and initiated the growth of the continental ice-cap during the Pleistocene period.

have been the region of the deepest accumulation of glacial ice; small wonder that the crust of the earth was depressed so much that it resulted in the formation of the depression now filled by the waters of Hudson Bay.

On the lowlands and plateaux of the Arctic coast erosion by massive glacial ice flow removed all of the unconsolidated soil and a good deal of the sedimentary rock cover, in places all of it. Great stretches of the Arctic coast consist of bare, polished rock surfaces which still bear the deep striations gouged into them by the boulders in the bottom of the flowing ice. In the island groups along the southeast coast of Hudson Bay, entire island surfaces are polished and grooved, with the grooves often a foot deep in the surface of the perfectly smooth rock. West of Hudson Bay and on Victoria Island the land is patterned into long ridges and alternating valleys that run for miles over the landscape making the land appear, when viewed from the air, like an immense ploughed field. Some of this ridge and valley pattern is due to the actual gouging out of the land, some of it to the fact that the glacial ice deposited the materials it scraped up into long rows of small drumlin hills, all oriented in the direction of the main glacial flow. One of the most spectacular forms of glacial deposition west of Hudson Bay is the esker. Eskers are formed from materials deposited in the beds of sub-glacial streams as the glacier melts away. Throughout the plains country west of Hudson Bay there are dozens of these miles long sand and gravel ridges that snake across the flat land in a variety of patterns.

Much of the Arctic surface is covered with glacial till, masses of unsorted rock, sand and gravel that have been deposited on the land in a haphazard fashion as the ice melted away. A till surface forms the typical tundra landscape, low in relief with very little systematic drainage, often patterned with hundreds of small, shallow lakes. In the early years after the retreat of the ice, glacial till was probably scattered in a more defined hill and valley arrangement, but long years of water and frost erosion has tended to flatten out the ridges and fill in the valleys helping to produce the level landscape of the tundra areas. Erratic boulders are everywhere on the land, often up to house-size boulders that have been carried to their present locations on the glacial ice and then left as the ice melted.

A major feature of the Arctic landscape is the raised beach-lines along the shores of the shallow seas and, inland west of Hudson Bay, around the tops of the high hills. The latter beaches, many of which are at heights of from six to nine hundred feet above present sea level, are thought to mark the successive levels of a large glacial lake that once formed in the interior country along the axis of the Thelon River-Baker Lake water system. From the air the hills appear to be ringed with concentric circles of water-washed reddish stones, splotched black with lichen and moss. The raised beaches along the sea-shores are the result of a gradual uplift of the land that occurred, and is still occurring, following the removal of the tremendous weight of the glacial ice. Geologists believe that the weight of the ice depressed the crust rocks downward into the viscous rock of the mantle of the earth. With the pressure removed the mantle is returning to its original shape, pushing the crust up with it.

The actual rate of the uplift has been accurately measured on the east coast of Pelly Bay in the central Arctic coast region. Radiocarbon dating of the remains of marine animals found buried beneath the beach sand of three uplifted terraces reveal that the first terrace, 175 feet above sea level, was cut about 7,160 years ago; the second terrace, now at 290 feet above sea level, was cut about 7,880 years ago; and the third terrace, now at 540 feet above sea level, was cut 8,370 years ago. These figures show that the uplift of the land immediately following the melting of the ice cover was quite rapid, about five inches per year. The rate slowed down to about two inches per year as the crust returned closer to the original equilibrium.

Geologists have calculated that the bottom of Hudson Bay, over which the ice accumulation was the deepest, will continue to rise in the future by as much as another 825 feet. This would mean the disappearance of Hudson and James Bays from the maps of Canada; the area would become a broad plain, drained by a major river system flowing north to the Arctic sea. The future benefits to the Arctic coast region from a continuing retreat of the glacial ice are many, not the least of which will be a second major river flowing from south to north, to an open polar sea!

Soft rock on the west coast of Hudson Bay, sculptured and polished by water and shifting ice, is gradually rising out of the sea.

6 THE TUNDRA BIOME—THE SOIL

In early spring of the year 1838 Thomas Simpson, accompanied by a small band of Indians of the northern bush, set off to the north from Great Bear Lake by sled. As the group made its way along the frozen river valleys the forests grew gradually sparser; the trees on which they depended for fuel became more stunted. Soon they reached areas where no trees grew at all; they moved out onto the open, treeless tundra across which bitter winds howled to bite into their bodies no longer protected by the wall of the northern bush. Moving through this edge-of-tree country about fifty miles northeast of Great Bear Lake they topped a rise and came down a long slope onto the ice surface of a narrow lake that stretched for miles off to the northwest where it joined another equally long and narrow lake, both rimmed on either side by low, snow-covered rock hills.

The land about them seemed absolutely devoid of life; only in a few sheltered hollows along the southern shore could they find small stands of stunted trees to use as wood for their fires and as supports for their tents. "Never have I seen a land so desolate and dismal as that which stretched before me," Simpson wrote later. He named the bodies of water the Dismal Lakes.

In later years another Arctic traveller reached the shores of the Dismal Lakes but he came from the north, travelling south after spending many months beyond the tree line on the ice surface of the sea along the northwest Arctic coast. "As I came over the hill and started down the slope toward the edge of the snow-covered lake I began to encounter small groups of trees standing upright in the shelter of tiny valleys. To my eyes, accustomed for many months to seeing only open, windswept north coast, this place seemed like a little bit of heaven, and I wondered how anyone could possibly have described these as—the Dismal Lakes."

This duality of appearance is characteristic of Arctic coast lands; eyes accustomed to the seemingly endless expanse of the northern bush, or to the lush growth of southern Canada, often see the treeless Arctic as a vast, empty and desolate wasteland in which grow only dwarf birch and willow bushes, a few acres of stunted grass, scattered patches of alpine flowers, and thousands of acres of nothing but moss and lichen-covered rock and gravel ridges. But others see the Arctic tundra as a high north wonderland—a land where flowers and plants thrive in the short but sunlit summer; where valley floors are carpeted with acres of cotton grass and sedges, alive with the buzz of insects and the flickering flights of bees and butterflies, supporting vast herds of caribou and smaller groups of musk ox, to say nothing of the lemmings and hares, and the thousands upon thousands of migratory birds that come north to nest and raise their young.

Whether the Arctic coast region is wasteland or wonderland is a subjective judgment, based entirely on human emotion and individual human experience. Within the more objective world of science the Arctic coast is neither wasteland nor wonderland; it is simply another area of the earth's surface within which distinctive life forms, especially adapted to the extreme seasonal variations in temperature, moisture and sunlight, have evolved and multiplied to fill many of the niches in the ecological structure that separates and unites all elements of the natural world. As the geologist divides the earth into regions, each a unit by virtue of its physical structure, so the ecologist divides the earth into realms, each a separate entity by virtue of its life forms.

North America, from Cape Columbia on northern Ellesmere Island south to the Tropic of Cancer, lies within the Nearctic Realm of nature, a huge land area that is further subdivided into a number of smaller and more cohesive regions called Biomes, each having its own volume of rain and snowfall, its own pattern of the seasons, its own relationship of day to night hours, all of which have combined to produce a unique selection of life forms that are found nowhere else in the world. The invisible barrier of climate defines the boundaries of a biome and, because it is climate that defines the main southern boundary of the Canadian Arctic triangle, the Arctic coast of Canada lies within a single natural unit—the tundra biome.

Range of temperature, hours of sunlight, amount of moisture, the cycle of the seasons determine the type of flora, and therefore the type of fauna, the tundra biome will support. Of basic importance to the flora is the type of soil within the region in which it can grow. Only lichens and some mosses are able to exist on bare rock; all other plants and shrubs must have soil in which to sink their root systems and from which to draw their sustenance. Some areas of the Arctic coast are completely without soil, such as the bare, ice-scraped rock islands in eastern Hudson Bay, and the stony beaches of some of the northern islands; but over most of the tundra biome the land has a surface covering made up of a mixture of soil and coarse rock particles, or of finer silt materials laid down by the rivers.

Most of the tundra soil is of glacial origin, a matrix of rock flour and rock particles stripped from the land by the scouring action of the flowing ice and then plastered onto the land wherever the ice flowed. The farther away from the glacial source, the finer the grind of the rock flour and the deeper the deposits of glacial soils become. Being within or close to the source areas for glacial ice the rock particles and soil of the Arctic coast received little grinding and, following the retreat of the ice, were deposited on the land surface in comparatively thin masses of completely unsorted materials—clay, gravel, sand, broken rock pieces, boulders of all sizes. Some of this material was later sorted and stratified by the water from the post-glacial lakes and by subsequent rain and frost action which combined to further disintegrate the rock particles and to carry the finer soil from the hilltops down onto the valley floors.

On the Arctic coast in summer the running water tends to wash the soil from the hilltops and ridges down into the valleys. But this process of erosion and deposition is very slow compared to such action in the temperate zone; for one thing the summer rainfall on the Arctic coast is light, consequently it cannot be a great agent of erosion. More important is the fact that the late spring and early summer melt period, the only time that a large volume of water runs down over the hillsides, occurs while much of the ground is still frozen solid and thus is resistant to active erosion by the running water. This has resulted in a surprisingly uniform distribution of the soil—on the hills it is coarse and thin, in the valleys it is finer and thicker. The coarse soil of the hills and ridges rapidly absorbs the moisture, the fine soils of the valleys retain it and hold it on or near the surface. Such conditions of soil and moisture have produced predictable results in the pattern of vegetative growth; on the hills plants and brush are sparse, restricted to the hardier types used to growing in dry soils, while in the valleys the vegetation is heavier and more varied, often made up of water-loving species.

Arctic soils are relatively infertile, especially deficient in nitrogen mainly as a result of low bacterial action; the bacteria being inhibited in their activity by the low temperatures in the soil. Experiments with Arctic plants have shown that the nitrogen levels of plants grown in cold soils are often equal to those of plants grown in warmer soils, but the low temperature reduces the assimilation of the nitrogen into organic compounds. Whenever nitrogen is introduced into Arctic soil, the resulting increase in the growth and quantity of the vegetation is quite startling. The carcass of a caribou or a musk ox, left on the ground to rot, will often be enough to initiate a luxuriant bed of local flora; the ancient campsites of Eskimo hunters of long ago are easily visible from the air, or from a boat coasting the shore,

After the spring and summer melt period, valley soil is fine-grained and retains moisture near the surface; vegetation is heavy and varied.

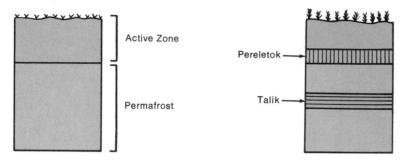

Much of the subsoil in the Arctic is permanently frozen the year round. Only the top few feet has a chance to thaw in summer.

The waters of Hudson Bay, or any large river or lake, serve as insulation and prevent formation of permafrost in ground below surface.

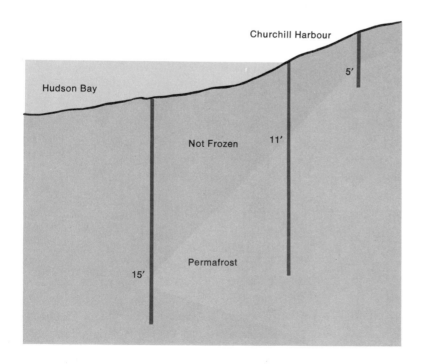

by the bright green of the local grasses and the dots of colour of the Arctic flowers that have grown up in the nitrogen-enriched soil. The slopes of the rocky hilltops on which the effluent pipelines of stations of the Distant Early Warning Line regularly discharge their waste materials, support growths of grass of a density and height quite unlike that found anywhere else in the area. The steep, rock faces of the many bird-nesting cliffs of the Arctic coast always support a lush and vivid growth of yellow, red and orange lichens; the tops of every small knoll in the tundra, favourite resting places of the larger birds, and denning places for foxes and ground squirrels, support luxuriant growths of grasses and Arctic flowers. And, however deficient the Arctic plants may be in nitrogen, they have an exceptionally high level of sugar thus making them highly nutritious food for the caribou and musk ox that roam the valleys, plains and plateaux.

The action of frost in the soil is a primary environmental factor in the growth and development of individual plants and of plant species. Not only have the Arctic plants had to adapt to a land of very low air temperatures and hard driving winter winds, they have had to contend with having their root systems encased in frozen materials for most of the year, subject to the break-up action of alternate thawing and freezing. During the autumn period the roots are often heaved up, torn and split by the tremendous power of the frost. Wherever the soil is unprotected by a cover of snow, which means on most of the hilltops and ridges of the Arctic coast, sudden, sharp drops in temperature in the autumn often split the ground wide open, tearing apart the root systems of the plants growing in the area of the crack. This results in the formation of greatly deformed root systems, if the plant is not killed outright, and it also causes the deformation of the stems of the upright perennials whenever the root is tipped, for the shoots will always grow vertically from the tilted stem.

The most widespread of the adverse ground conditions due to frost that must be met and conquered by Arctic plants is that of permafrost—the permanently frozen ground that extends down for varying distances beneath all the Arctic coast land surface. Permafrost underlies as much as one-fifth of all land areas of the world, principally in the northern hemisphere; in Canada between forty and fifty per cent of the land is underlain by permafrost. In the southern sectors of the Arctic coast region permafrost extends down for as little as a few dozen feet, while in the high Arctic islands it is known to penetrate more than twelve hundred feet below the surface.

The origin of permafrost is still not well understood. Most scientists agree that it probably made its appearance in northern North America during the cold periods of the Pleistocene period, although not necessarily beneath the land when it was actually under glacial ice; the thick cover of ice and snow would provide an insulating blanket superimposed on any frost that may have existed already in the ground. During the periods of fluctuating warmth and cold of the Pleistocene there must have been corresponding fluctuations in the depth and extent of the areas of permafrost; it may have disappeared altogether during the warmer periods.

Today permafrost in both Canada and Russia is forming in some areas, retreating in others; it is not present beneath the floors of the large Arctic lakes and rivers, even in the high Arctic. There is no permafrost under the bed of the Mackenzie River nor under the floor of Lake Hazen on northern Ellesmere Island, and it is thought to be absent beneath the waters of Hudson Bay for it is known to thin out very quickly seaward from the thickness of about 140 feet it attains in the vicinity of Churchill, Manitoba. But, whenever an island forms in a lake or a sandbar builds up in a river, permafrost begins to form in the soil immediately. Permafrost is known to form in southern Canada; not long ago it was discovered within the city limits of Edmonton, Alberta, when a large icehouse, in use over a long period of time, was dismantled and the ground beneath found to be frozen down to a depth of several feet with every indication that it had been permanently frozen during all the period that the ice-house stood above.

The formation of permafrost in soil is governed by a number of inter-related factors—air temperature, amount of precipitation, degree of cloud cover of the sky, direction of prevailing winds, the texture and water content of the vegetation above the ground all play important roles. Theoretically it can form whenever the mean annual temperature at the earth's surface falls below 32 degrees Fahrenheit, but in fact it does not begin to form until the temperature falls several degrees lower than this, due mainly to differing local soil and weather conditions. The actual rate of growth of permafrost has been observed in the

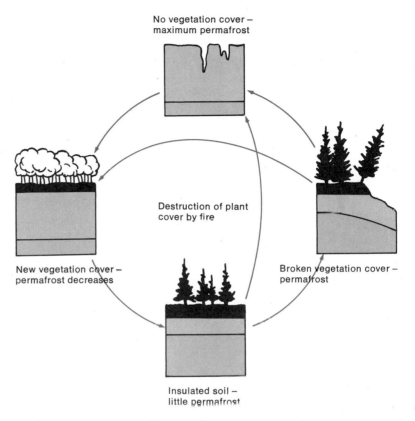

Surface vegetation provides another source of insulation, preventing the ground from freezing into a state of permafrost.

Arctic buildings are constructed on a cover of insulating material, to prevent the building sinking due to heat melting the permafrost.

area of the mouth of the Nelson River on the lower west coast of Hudson Bay. During the construction of the Hudson Bay Railway, which originally was to have had its northern terminus at Port Nelson and not at Churchill, a swamp with an unfrozen bed was drained. During the following winter frost penetrated the ground beneath the drained area to a depth of eight feet and did not melt the following summer. The second winter it deepened its penetration to twenty feet and in the third winter extended down to thirty feet which was the lowest depth of the permafrost for this area. At thirty feet it stopped forming, having reached the level at which the local seasonal changes in temperature had diminished with depth to the point where no new frost would form.

Near the surface the permafrost is divided into two layers, a deep layer that never melts (in contemporary terms), and a thin surface layer that thaws each year during the summer. The thawed layer of the permafrost is the "active" layer, and it is in this thin film of thawed soil that most Arctic vegetation grows. The active layer can be as thin as a few inches or as thick as a few feet; on an average within the Arctic coast region its base in summer would be about twelve to eighteen inches below the surface. Wherever the active layer is shallow the frozen ground near the surface represses all deep-rooted plants for their roots cannot penetrate the permafrost, although they can exist quite close to its upper surface. Plant roots growing near the permafrost often have an ovoid cross-section because of the greater amount of annual growth on the upper side of the root away from the frost surface.

Permafrost also affects vegetation through its influence on the drainage patterns of the Arctic coast; its upper surface provides a water-impervious base close to the surface of the land confining drainage to the surface layer, making the low lying regions of the tundra wet and bog-like, eliminating from such areas all but the water-oriented species. Were it not for the permafrost base beneath such land all surface moisture would drain away and great stretches of the Arctic coast would revert back to barren desert. It is paradoxical that the icy lid of permafrost keeps much of the Arctic tundra in bloom during the short summer.

One result of the trapping of large volumes of water in the thin layer of soil above the lid of the permafrost is soil creep or soilfluction. Soil creep occurs in southern Canada, the most readily visible example of this earth phenomenon is the slippage of the surface layers of earth on the newly graded embankments of the highways, where large masses of sod and soil often slide downhill before the roots of the grasses have a chance to take firm hold and keep the soil in place. On the Arctic coast soil creep occurs when the thin layer of soil in the active layer becomes heavily saturated with water in the summer and then slides gently downhill, coasting on the frozen top of the underlying permafrost. On gentle slopes this results in the development of a step pattern on the hillside; soil creep can occur on hills with a gradient as little as two percent and the resulting step configuration has a decided effect on the plant growth; the drier swells of soil support a different type of vegetation than the wet troughs between. In the high Arctic Islands soil creep often results in minor, sometimes major, earth movements.

Not only do Arctic plants have to contend with the violent freezing action of the surface soil each year and with the permanently frozen ground close to their roots, they have to adapt to a number of freeze-thaw phenomena that result in the formation of the surface soil into distinctive ground patterns. Throughout the Arctic coast region much of the land is clearly marked off in series of more or less symmetrical forms—circles, stripes, steps, polygons—that are the result of intensive frost action, the most common of which is the polygon. Best seen from above, polygon soil formations pattern great areas of the plateaux and the gentle slopes of the valleys. Rarely do they appear singly; usually they form an interconnected grid often covering wide stretches of ground dozens of square miles in extent.

Permafrost is both a negative and a positive factor on the Arctic coast—negative because of its deleterious effect on plant growth; positive because if it wasn't for the permafrost floor supporting the mixture of thawed soil and water on the surface of the land in summer there would be no vegetation at all over large stretches of the Arctic coast. In turn, the Arctic vegetation helps the permafrost near the surface by acting as an insulator from the heat of the sun's rays, preserving the permafrost table. Thus, the killing cold of the permafrost and the gentle heat mat created by the Arctic flora exist in symbiotic harmony, enemies yet friends, each playing a part in the preservation of natural life in a land dominated by cold and ice.

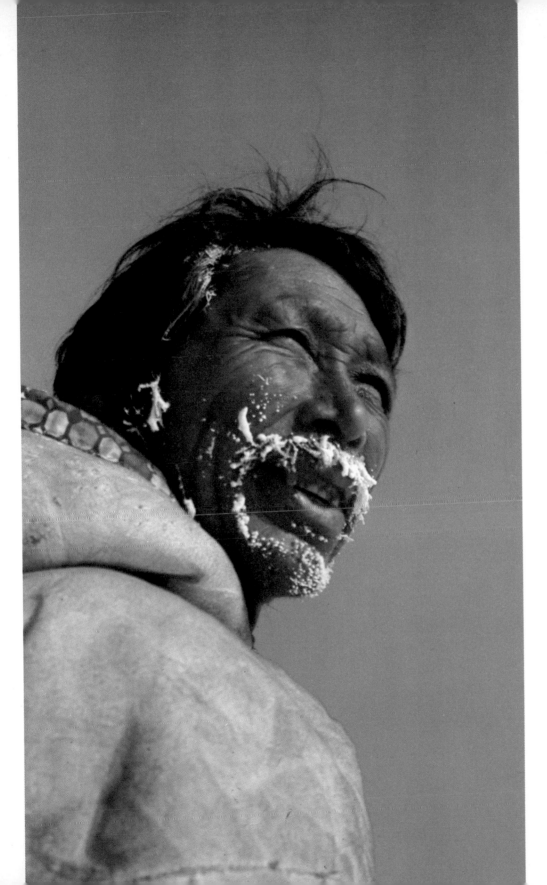

NATIVE MAN

Centuries ago, just how many centuries no one is quite sure, the mammal, man, moved into his ecological niche in the tundra biome of North America. He came from the east, out of the great Oriental branch of humankind, to migrate first over the dry land that connected Asia to North America about 10,000 years ago, and later across the narrow channel of Bering Strait, formed when the rising waters of the world's oceans, replenished by the melting of the glacial ice, encroached upon the lowland. Man came to northern North America as a hunter, already well adapted to life in the cold; a tundra nomad who gradually drifted along the coast on the top of the world until he occupied almost every corner of the emerging Arctic coast from Alaska to Greenland and as far south as Hudson Bay and the Gulf of the St. Lawrence River.

57

Note: Eskimo groups in black type
Indian tribes in red type
Areas of Eskimo settlement shaded purple

A collision of cultures

Eskimo hunters killed other Eskimo hunters
but, on the Arctic coasts of Canada, Eskimo
groups never engaged in inter-tribal war.
The ethic of the true Arctic coast hunter was
one of peace and understanding, a balanced
quiet broken only by the occasional family
feud and murder. However, all Eskimo groups
lived permanently in a state of war with the
neighbouring Indian tribes, from the mouth
of the St. Lawrence to the far off Beaufort
Sea. This warfare was so intense that the
Eskimo people were unable to colonize the
more hospitable lands to the south. Only
the barren Arctic was left to these early
colonizers from Asia.

*Naskapi Indians attack an Eskimo encampment
on the southeast coast of Ungava Bay.*

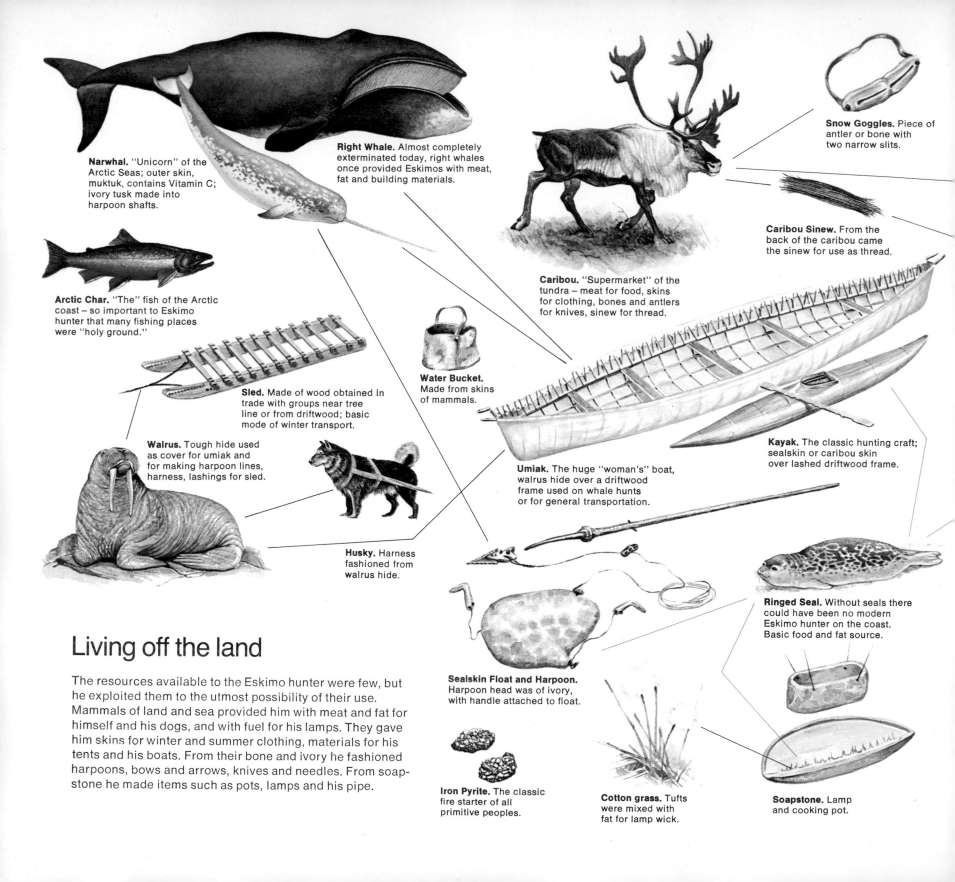

Narwhal. "Unicorn" of the Arctic Seas; outer skin, muktuk, contains Vitamin C; ivory tusk made into harpoon shafts.

Right Whale. Almost completely exterminated today, right whales once provided Eskimos with meat, fat and building materials.

Snow Goggles. Piece of antler or bone with two narrow slits.

Caribou Sinew. From the back of the caribou came the sinew for use as thread.

Caribou. "Supermarket" of the tundra – meat for food, skins for clothing, bones and antlers for knives, sinew for thread.

Arctic Char. "The" fish of the Arctic coast – so important to Eskimo hunter that many fishing places were "holy ground."

Sled. Made of wood obtained in trade with groups near tree line or from driftwood; basic mode of winter transport.

Water Bucket. Made from skins of mammals.

Kayak. The classic hunting craft; sealskin or caribou skin over lashed driftwood frame.

Walrus. Tough hide used as cover for umiak and for making harpoon lines, harness, lashings for sled.

Umiak. The huge "woman's" boat, walrus hide over a driftwood frame used on whale hunts or for general transportation.

Husky. Harness fashioned from walrus hide.

Ringed Seal. Without seals there could have been no modern Eskimo hunter on the coast. Basic food and fat source.

Living off the land

The resources available to the Eskimo hunter were few, but he exploited them to the utmost possibility of their use. Mammals of land and sea provided him with meat and fat for himself and his dogs, and with fuel for his lamps. They gave him skins for winter and summer clothing, materials for his tents and his boats. From their bone and ivory he fashioned harpoons, bows and arrows, knives and needles. From soapstone he made items such as pots, lamps and his pipe.

Sealskin Float and Harpoon. Harpoon head was of ivory, with handle attached to float.

Iron Pyrite. The classic fire starter of all primitive peoples.

Cotton grass. Tufts were mixed with fat for lamp wick.

Soapstone. Lamp and cooking pot.

Wolverine. Fur of wolverine prized as trim for parka hood because ice and frost can be quickly beaten free.

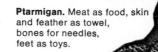

Ptarmigan. Meat as food, skin and feather as towel, bones for needles, feet as toys.

Needle. Made from ptarmigan bone.

Black Guillemot. Provided the hunter with eggs and meat in late spring.

Musk Ox. Hides used as covers on sleeping platform of snow houses; cups and ladles were carved from horns.

Spool. Fish jigger was a standard part of hunting equipment of every Eskimo.

Ladle. Carved from soapstone.

Bow. Musk ox horn tough and sinewy; ideal for bow. Plaited sinew for string, caribou antler for arrow.

Sealskin parka or old caribou-skin parka
Sealskin trousers
Sealskin boots
Sealskin mitts
Socks of bird or rabbit skin

Two complete suits of caribou skin – inner worn with fur next to body, outer with fur to outside; clothes light, airy and extremely warm.

Spoon. shaped from musk ox horn.

Summer Dress.

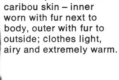

Knives. The snow knife, essential to Eskimo survival could be made from a variety of materials.

Winter Dress.

Sleeping Robe. Heavy musk ox skin was used on sleeping platform.

Woman's Knife. Ulu, the woman's knife, for cutting and scraping.

Catkin tinder. Shown in pouch.

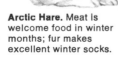

Arctic Hare. Meat is welcome food in winter months; fur makes excellent winter socks.

Arctic fox. Almost worthless to Eskimo hunter but source of approximately 90% of income of trapper.

Arctic Willow. Provides tinder.

Polar Bear. Every part utilized except liver which contains too much Vitamin A, and is extremely toxic to humans.

Ermine. Of little use to Eskimo hunter; of value to trapper for trade in store.

Ground Squirrel. In times of starvation ground squirrels provided an alternate source of food.

Eskimo architecture

The Eskimo snowhouse, although found only in the central Canadian Arctic, has come to symbolize Arctic architecture. In order to conserve heat the interior of the dwelling was at different levels—the floor was below ground level, allowing little cold air to enter, while the top of the sleeping bench was at a height greater than entrance level to take advantage of warmer air. The snowhouse tended to be warmer if built on sea ice since the water was not as cold as permafrost on land. The sleeping bench was covered with willow branches and musk ox skins. Body warmth and heat from the lamps kept the inside of the house warm enough to allow a minimum of clothing to be worn.

The Eskimo's most ingenious dwelling was the winter snowhouse. First he found a snowdrift of just the right hardness, from which he cut blocks of snow, laying them in a circle. By back-cutting some of these first blocks he was able to start an unending upward and inward-leaning spiral, building his home around him as he went, not cutting his way out until the final "key" block was inserted and the house was complete.

In summer the hunters made tents of sealskin or caribou skin held upright by driftwood or whalebone poles. Some Eskimos made winter homes from blocks of peat-like turf, or dug semi-caves in hillsides and roofed them over by stretching sealskins over a whalebone frame.

Eskimo hunter scans the sea-ice surface looking for sleeping seals.

Sled dogs wait patiently at floe edge of ice as hunter retrieves seal.

Hunters of the Arctic coast

The earliest known migrants to come to the Arctic coast of Canada were proto-Eskimos, called by scientists the Pre-Dorset people. Seasonal nomads, the Pre-Dorsets hunted seals and walrus on and in the sea. First appearing in Alaska about 3500 B.C., by 2000 B.C. they had spread all the way east to Greenland where further expansion was halted by the wide expanse of the Greenland Sea. For 3000 years, until roughly 800 B.C., the Pre-Dorsets hunted and travelled throughout the Arctic coast region of Canada, gradually evolving into the Dorset culture people, originators of the snow-house or igloo. Dorset hunters reigned supreme on the north coast until about 900 A.D. at which time a thin wave of immigrants of a different Arctic culture, Thule, began to drift slowly along the coast from Alaska to completely replace the Dorsets as the dominant group. The Eskimo hunter of today is a direct descendant of the Thule people still wedded largely to life on the edge of the sea.

Hunter removes seal skin with a "snow" knife; the skin is used for clothing, boots, tents or kayak cover.

Bent in position with a harpoon, this hunter waits for a seal to rise up in the breathing hole hidden beneath the snow.

Using a white canvass screen to camouflage his dark figure, this hunter stalks and kills a seal sleeping on the ice.

Lichens grow well on the smooth surface of glacial-scoured rock.

PART THREE / **PLANT LIFE**

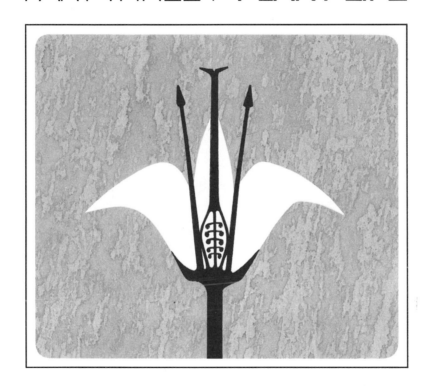

7 THE TUNDRA BIOME—THE FLORA

The myth of the year-round frozen north dies hard, for cold is our enemy and a cold climate the sign of a disordered land; only gradually are we coming to recognize that, despite its long background of development in a world of warmth, life on earth has adapted to the condition of cold in the same way that it has adapted to the condition of aridity that produced the deserts, to the condition of excessive wetness that produced the bog and swamps. Hunting man developed clothing and shelter that enabled him to live in the coldest of Arctic coast lands, providing at least a part of the land was free of permanent ice and he could find food; mammals of land and sea developed special physiological features that enabled them to resist the debilitating effect of extreme cold on their warm bodies. But all such adaptations among the fauna pale in comparison with the special traits developed by the flora that enabled certain plant species to live and propagate their kind under the severest conditions found anywhere on the face of the earth. On planet earth, where the factor of continual change is the one constant element, adaptability is the key to ultimate survival and nowhere is this quality better illustrated than by the flora of the Arctic world.

On display at the Plant Research Institute of the Experimental Farm in Ottawa are a number of tiny plants that are probably the oldest growing flora in the world today—Arctic Lupines grown from seeds found embedded in the permanently frozen soil of the northwest Arctic coast where they had lain undisturbed since they were placed in an ancient burrow by Arctic lemmings more than 10,000 years ago. For all of this immensely long period of time the seeds had been frozen, surrounded by frozen soil. Yet, brought forth into the light, supplied with heat and moisture, they were still capable of reproducing their kind. For 10,000 years the seeds had remained in a state of suspended animation, dormant yet viable, awaiting only the right set of conditions to spring to life again. "And," states Dr. A. E. Porsild, the recently retired chief of the National Museum's Herbarium and a long time researcher and collector of Arctic flora, "there is no reason to believe that there aren't seeds in even older deposits in the north. They could go back 1,000,000 years, to the beginning of the ice age."

How it is possible for life to withstand freezing for 10,000 years and then grow again as though nothing had happened, we do not know as yet. But it happens, and it is significant that it happens in the world of the flora, the plants that stand at the beginning of the food chains that link all living creatures together in a state of complete inter-dependency; without plants

EDIBLE PLANTS

No true Arctic plant is poisonous and all are possible sources of vitamins, yet the short growing season and the nomadic life of most Arctic peoples have kept their dependance on plants as a source of food to a minimum. These plants, however, are all eaten when available and are especially valuable to non-native peoples who do not eat the internal organs of animals and miss the prime source of vitamins that is available to the Eskimos.

Fernweed

Sweet Coltsfoot

Mountain Sorrel

Arctic Sourdock

there would be no mammals, no man. Freezing will kill all fauna, permanent ice and perpetual cold will drive them from a region; but such conditions cannot completely kill or drive out all the flora. Most Arctic plants can be frozen stiff and then continue growing without any ill effect the moment they are thawed out; certain seeds have the remarkable ability to hibernate, to lie dormant through thousands, perhaps millions of years of freezing. Surely this must be the ultimate in adaptation for survival of species in a cold land.

To the gardener in southern Canada, often struggling to grow flowers and plants under next to ideal conditions, with varying degrees of success, the idea that plants and bushes thrive on the Arctic coast of Canada, a land under the control of ice, might seem a little strange. However, soil needed for plant life exists in many areas of the north coast, all the way up to the farthest north land areas on Ellesmere Island. Almost everywhere on the Arctic coast temperatures in the short summer climb high enough to provide a short growing period that is immeasurably assisted by the fact that the sun shines on the land for twenty-four hours of the day in many localities, helping plant life survive and thrive. But, in order to live and propagate, plants have had to develop species with characteristics of growth adapted to the rigorous conditions, plants with life cycles geared to a land where for the greater portion of the year they must lie

dormant in or on the frozen ground while surface temperatures drop to fifty and sixty below zero and icy winds from off icy seas sweep over them; plants that can put down short roots into the thin layer of cold, thawed ground above the permanently frozen soil; plants capable of absorbing moisture mainly during the brief period of spring and early summer thaw.

On the Arctic coast of Canada there are five types of flora—lichens, mosses, grasses, plants and shrubs—that grow in three distinct community groupings, the tundra community, the rock and gravel hill community, the seashore community. On the seashore are the salt-tolerant grasses and sedges of the tidal flats, sandwort and sea pink; on the rock and gravel hills are lichens, mosses and cushion-type plants such as the saxifrages, plus the hardiest of the colonizing plants, the Arctic poppy. The tundra supports the lushest growth and the most varied Arctic vegetation; valleys carpeted in thick grasses, banks of rivers and streams lined with dwarf shrubs such as creeping birch and dwarf willow, slopes of the hills cloaked with the berry-bearing bushes interspersed with clumps of Arctic heather and vast areas carpeted with caribou moss.

With its great variety of plants and shrubs the tundra goes through a seasonal colour cycle that is a counterpart of the cycle in the deciduous forests of central and southern Canada. In spring the land is white with snow. Very quickly it turns to

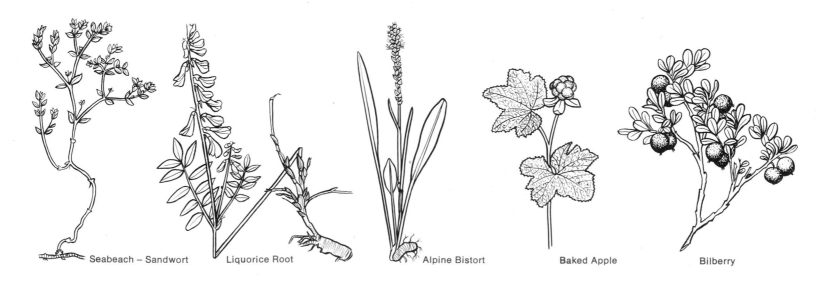

Seabeach – Sandwort   Liquorice Root   Alpine Bistort   Baked Apple   Bilberry

69

brown as the snow melts away; then the brown coloration is relieved by splotches of green as the grasses renew their growth. Tiny splashes of bright colours appear wherever the flowers bloom; fields of white Arctic cotton grass flutter in the breeze.

There are almost no annual species of Arctic plants, the growing season so short that the normal life processes of the annual plants cannot be completed in one season. Almost all plants are perennials, able to spring into life quickly following a long period—nine to ten months of the year—of winter hibernation. Many of the plants lie dormant through the winter with seed in an advanced state of germination; many have seed pods covered with fluffy down for insulation against the heavy frost of the winter. In early summer, often before the snow has left the land, the plant will come to flower under the warming effect of the twenty-four hour daylight period. All plants spring to life, bloom quickly, turn colour and then go into hibernation again. This factor of very quick, yet very low, annual growth rate dominates all development of flora in the Arctic coast region.

The ubiquitous lichen is the humble plant of a not-so-humble land, a flat, rootless growth that flourishes where no other plant could possibly grow. Lichens grow almost anywhere on earth, their advance halted only by perpetual snow and ice, but they are especially well suited to life on the Arctic coast because of their capacity to withstand cold and lack of moisture, and because of their fondness for subsisting on naked rock. Lichens are among the first plants to move into barren ground and often they enable higher forms of vegetation to obtain a foothold on the new land.

Lichens are actually a composite of two separate entities linked together in a strange partnership; one part of the lichen is a fungus which produces acids that disintegrate the rock on which it grows, thus supplying minerals to its other part which is an algae. The algae, in turn, supplies the fungus with organic materials without which it would not be able to live. Lichens can be black or green, yellow or brown, bright red or bright orange; growing on the rocks of the Arctic coast they provide the land with much of its colour, both summer and winter. Many lichens are edible; the most important is the reindeer moss, *Cladonia*, which is sometimes mistaken for a moss but is actually a lichen, the main winter food for the great herds of caribou that roam the tundra valleys.

Although the plant life of the Arctic coast is far too sparse and too dwarfed to be considered as a food supply to man, all Arctic plants are edible and contain varying amounts of vitamins, proteins, sugars and starches. It is possible to eat any Arctic plant that looks at all appetizing without fear of being poisoned—there are no poisonous plants, no poisonous mushrooms, roots or berries. The easiest to pick and eat, and certainly the most wholesome to man, are the small fruits of the various bushes found everywhere in the sheltered valleys of the mainland and Baffin Island. Most of these berries are very hardy; they are not damaged by freezing on the branch, in fact freezing often improves the flavour. They can be collected from under the snow in the winter and even the next spring after the snow has melted away.

The leaves and stems of a number of flowering Arctic plants can be eaten like a salad, or used to make soups or flavour stews. Roots of other plants serve the same purpose. Leaves of certain plants can be boiled to produce a drink; even the lowly lichen can be boiled in water to jell into a nutritious and readily digestible food. Many different kinds of edible puff balls and mushrooms grow throughout the Arctic, especially in the grasslands of the tundra. Along the sea coast there are edible species of seaweed and marine algae.

A favourite of the Eskimo hunter is Arctic sorrel grass, a plant that looks like a miniature rhubarb and grows everywhere in the country north of the tree line, from the tundra of the mainland interior to the mountain valleys of northern Ellesmere Island. Sorrel grass stems and flowers can grow to a height of almost a foot, but four to six inches is closer to normal and the leaves are often as big as twenty-five cent pieces. Leaves and stems are succulent and juicy, with the strong acid taste of "green" apples. Cooked, the leaves resemble spinach and taste not unlike that vegetable; the liquid from the boiling can be sweetened with a little sugar, cooled and drunk as a refreshing summer beverage. Sorrel grass is the only plant of the Arctic that I have ever seen Eskimo adults actually collect and eat as a part of the summer food supply. When hunting on the sea in summer with my Eskimo "father," Idlouk, a small sugar sack was always stuffed into the bow of the kayak and often we would go ashore at certain locations near good sealing and whaling waters to collect the sorrel grass that grew in abundance.

THE ARCTIC IN BLOOM

A few inches, at best a foot or two, beneath these flowering Arctic white heather and Lapland rhododendron, lies the icy mantle of the permafrost, permanently frozen ground extending down as much as 1200 feet below the surface of the land. Each summer in the thin, thawed layer of soil above the permafrost, the Arctic plants burst into bloom to dot the treeless tundra with patches of brilliant colour. Battered by icy winds and often dusted with summer snow, their root systems branching out horizontally, Arctic plants, mosses and shrubs flourish wherever there is soil and water to support growth.

Much of the Arctic coast is rock, but lichens grow almost everywhere.

The broad leaves of Salix reticulata *soak up the 24-hour sun.*

A miniature "forest" of tiny Arctic plants flourishes here.

Summer splendour

In the short Arctic coast summer the treeless land
comes alive. On cloudy days the land is a monotone of
gray or brown, but when the sun shines throughout
the 24-hour long day, rock and earth is patterned
with vibrant colour—the yellow and green and orange
of lichens growing on the rocks, the yellow of the
Arctic poppy, the purple of the saxifrage. Sections of
tundra are not unlike parts of southern Alberta—foot
high grass bends under the wind; scrub bush grows in
the sheltered waterways; bees and butterflies flit from
flower to flower; spiders dart across the springy turf.
Each year the tundra goes through a seasonal colour
cycle—from late winter white, to brown, to green and
then to the brilliant reds, yellows and golds of autumn.
Then, as the sun slips lower on the southern horizon,
cold re-establishes control over the land. Lakes and
rivers freeze; snow covers the tiny tundra "forest."
It will be nine months before the plants are seen again.

The caribou could not exist without the lichen, or caribou "moss."

Huge patches of purple saxifrage splash brilliant colour in the area.

Arctic willow pods are protected from the cold by fluffy down.

Arctic cotton grass is used as wick material for seal oil lamps.

The bright yellow marsh fleabane (above) is a common and beautiful edible herb.

Most Arctic flowers, like the delicate-looking Stellaria ciliatosepala (above) and the brightly-hued rhododendron (below) hug the ground to escape the bitter winds.

A burst of colour

Summer in the Arctic does not get as hot as the winter gets cold, but the region does have 24-hours of sunshine, and earth and water. Nourished by these elements, plant life grows and has developed many special features to overcome the relatively low summer temperatures and chilling winds. Temperatures within the brightly-coloured flower petals are several degrees warmer than those in the few white flowers which have survived. Many plants have hair covered leaves and stalks, to help along an earlier flowering, while others can freeze stiff and then thaw out to resume growth without suffering any ill effects.

The hardy Arctic poppy (right) sends its flowers 6 to 12 inches above the soil.

8 FLORAL ADAPTATION TO THE COLD

Of the various factors affecting the growth and development of plants in the Arctic the most important is temperature during the critical weeks of late spring and early summer. In vegetation the onset of photosynthesis takes place at a temperature of about 43° Fahrenheit. Because of the generally low Arctic air temperatures in summer and because of the further effect of chilling due to the cold winds that blow over the treeless land, Arctic flora has a hard time keeping warm enough for photosynthesis to take place. To overcome this difficulty plants have developed a number of special features.

Arctic plants and shrubs grow close to the ground where they are able to escape some of the effect of wind-chill but, more important, they create for themselves a tiny "forest" of vegetation about four or five inches high which may cover acres, as in the tundra valleys, or mere inches, as in the single, cushion-type plant. Within this "forest" temperatures are considerably higher than those found generally in the area. This permits the metabolic processes of the plants to proceed at a much faster pace than would be possible otherwise. In effect, the Arctic flora has adapted to the condition of summer cold by creating its own micro-environment within which the range of summer temperatures will differ from those of the open air only a few inches above.

In a recorded instance, with the air at minus 12 degrees Centigrade, the temperature within the mass of dead leaves of a saxifrage plant was plus 3.5 degrees Centigrade and within a dark clump of heavy cluster moss it stood at plus 10 degrees Centigrade. While these actual temperature differences may not be great compared to those created in the temperate or tropic zones, within the Arctic tundra biome a relatively minor increase in temperature within and around the plants is highly significant to processes accustomed to operating at close to borderline conditions most of the time.

There is a specialization on the part of some plant species that has seen the development of another micro-environment, one that exists beneath the many snowbanks that remain on the ground long after the general snow cover has disappeared. Certain plants are able to begin growth while still buried beneath as much as three to four feet of snow. This may not be quite the hardship it seems; plants buried under the snow have a great deal of extra protection from cold during the critical stages of spring and early summer growth, when unseasonably low air temperatures accompanied by high winds can arrest growth and even destroy the plant. Some Arctic species can remain in a state of arrested development while buried under snow banks for two years or more. Under such conditions, many physiological processes do not occur but the large carbohydrate reserves in the plant roots enable them to survive until the ground above becomes free of snow again.

It is known that the acceleration of the physiological processes in plants through temperature changes, such as occur during diurnal cycles and through the variations of cloud cover in the sky, is much greater within the lower range of temperatures than in the higher values. Although temperatures are relatively low on the Arctic coast they do show significant gradients within the day-night time cycle and Arctic plants are able to carry out growth and development patterns much faster than do their cousins in the temperate and tropic zones of the world. As well, temperature gradients on a south-facing slope in the Arctic will have an even greater variation within the lower range and will tend to produce and support a greater variety and quantity of plants. Almost all Arctic flowers are brightly coloured and the temperatures within the coloured petals are between five and six degrees warmer than the temperatures within the petals of the few flowers that are white; white flowers have failed in their adaptation to an extremely cold climate while brightly coloured flowers have succeeded in keeping warm enough to propagate and spread. As well, most Arctic flowers have quite large blooms in relation to the size of the vegetative shoots. This factor of large size is important to all life in a cold land, flora and fauna, for large size generally assists any organism in its flight to counter the effect of cold.

A good proportion of Arctic plants have a thick cuticle and an abundance of hair on the leaves and stalks both of which raise temperatures about the plant by trapping long-wave radiation, allowing much earlier flowering than would otherwise be

Labrador Tea

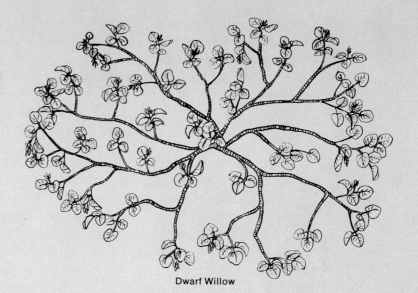

Dwarf Willow

All Arctic plants must retain enough heat to enable photo-synthesis to take place. The chilling Arctic winds and the short periods of warm sunlight have made many special adaptations necessary. The Labrador tea is a low-growing plant, with its leaves covered beneath by a dense rust-coloured felt. The small leathery leaves serve as storage for winter food and are resistent to the drying effects of the wind. The mountain avens form a clump for warmth but this plant endures exposed winter sites where it does not have the insulation of snow cover, so that it can begin growth before the snow has melted. The dwarf willow hugs the ground to escape the deadly wind chill. The hardy leaves are hairy on both surfaces to retain all available warmth. The purple saxifrage is extremely adaptable, can make optimum use of the environment and is the most common flower of the northern region.

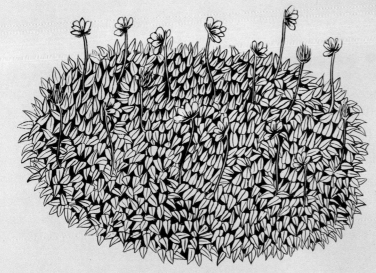

Mountain Avens

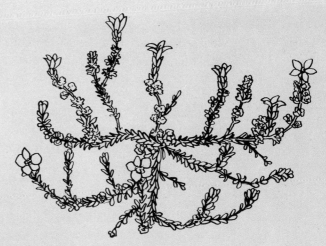

Purple Saxifrage

possible. Many have a cushion-growth that enables them to conserve heat and take full advantage of the higher surface temperatures and reduced wind speeds within the cushion. Still others disdain to adopt any special configuration, they merely freeze stiff during cold snaps and then thaw out to resume growth without seeming to suffer any ill effects. It is not at all unusual for Arctic plants to be frozen in air temperatures of minus three degrees Centigrade and be covered with rime ice, then to thaw without sign of frost damage. Some species are able to arrest development and over-winter in any stage, ready to continue the growing process the following summer. Flowers of such plants take two years to develop, with the initiation of the flower in the first year and the expansion into the full flower the next. Such species are poised and ready for instant flowering in the second spring, often bursting forth before the snow cover has disappeared from the land.

All Arctic flora has a very low annual rate of growth; this is particularly true of the shrubs such as the willow and birch and juniper. Part of the reason for this is the generally low temperatures on the Arctic coast, but another important factor is the wind. Wind-chill is as hard on plants as it is on man; as a result Arctic brush hugs the ground where the velocity of the wind is less and the effect of the wind isn't as great. In sheltered valleys along the well-watered river courses willow will grow upright, reaching heights of three to four feet in such valleys along the north shore of Baker Lake; but on the bare, windswept ridges willow and birch creep along the ground, nowhere rising up more than an inch or two, often ten to fifteen feet long, and very old. Counts of annual growth rings, which can be seen only under a microscope, have revealed such bushes to be as much as four hundred years old.

From present knowledge it appears that not every year on the Arctic coast is suitable for seed production and germination. The pattern seems to be one of considerable production of seedlings over a few years followed by several years during which few, if any, seedlings take root. As yet not a great deal is known about pollination among Arctic plants although it is known that self-pollination is an important method, as would be expected in such a severe environment where little time is to be lost if the plant is to propagate and grow. There are bees, flies, moths and butterflies on the Arctic coast and indications are that plants depend on them for cross-pollination which helps to ensure a much greater genetic diversity within the plant communities than would be possible otherwise. Some Arctic plants do not conform to the general hug-the-ground pattern but extend flowers and seed pods upright on straight stems in order to take advantage of the Arctic summer winds in carrying the seeds far and wide across the land. In addition a number of species do not drop seeds until after the first falls of snow in the autumn; the seeds are transported by the later shifting and melting of the snow cover.

The high frequency of plants with asexual seed production ensures the continued propagation of new and vigorous types and also permits a rapid (for the Arctic) build-up of well adapted, genetically similar plants. Such plants are no doubt the first to colonize newly available land areas such as those laid bare by the retreat of glacial ice. Often they will move into a new area before the lichens and mosses have taken hold, and they will continue to grow on land surfaces that are under the shadow of massive walls of ice. The outwash plain of the Thompson and White glaciers is a scene of cold, hard beauty, a section of land about to be engulfed by a huge mass of glacial ice that is bearing down over it relentlessly, year after year. Across the front of the ice cliff of the Thompson glacier a wild stream runs rampant throughout the short summer, tearing at the rocks and gravel of the plain, ripping off great chunks of its banks that vanish into the swift waters and are carried off to the sea. Down from off the glacial tongue icy winds pour their never-ending streams of cold air across the plain, keeping the temperature at the base of the ice cliff near the freezing point all summer long, helping to make this place a most unlikely spot to find anything growing, except the wall of glacial ice.

Yet, about ten yards from the eroding bank of the glacial stream, a mere fifty yards from the face of the fifty foot high wall of ice, an infinitesimal patch of colour breaks the fierce monotony of brown and white; a tiny, yellow Arctic poppy bobs gently in the icy wind, completely contemptuous of the coarse rock and gravel soil at its base, equally contemptuous of the wall of ice rearing high overhead. Surely this little flower must share with the hardy seed of the Arctic lupine the honour of the near-ultimate in adaptability for survival in a land controlled by ice and cold.

THE LIVING ARCTIC

The wolf (above) is a predator, feeding mainly on caribou meat, but he can live well on ground squirrels, lemmings and birds' eggs. Seals must have air to breathe yet they live all winter in the sea under six feet of ice. The polar bear is a land animal but spends most of his life in the sea. Musk ox resemble, but are not related to, buffalo or ox, nor do they smell of musk; they are relics of a bygone age, descended in unbroken line from species first evolved one million years ago.

The sea in summer

Beneath the floating ice-pan of the Arctic sea in summer swims an occasional Greenland right whale, hunted almost to extinction by the rapacious whalers fifty years ago. More numerous are the Belugas – white whales – ten to fifteen feet long, toothed, slate-blue in colour when born but turning milk-white by the time they are four years old. In the open water near the floating pack swims the narwhal, unicorn of the Arctic seas. About the same size as the white whale, the narwhal is mottled black and white on the back and sides, whitish underneath. The male narwhal develops from its left upper jaw a spirally-grooved tusk of ivory that is often eight to nine feet long and can weigh as much as thirty pounds. The odd male has two tusks, one much shorter than the other. Even rarer is a female narwhal with a developed tusk. Swimming in the sea or sunning themselves on the floating ice are ringed seals, the layer of fat about their rotund bodies so thin in summer that they will not float when killed. Cleaving the dark green water of the open sea is the head of a polar bear as it swims strongly towards the distant shore. The polar bear paddles with front feet only when swimming; hind feet simply trail out behind. Above the water surface, and at the steep rock cliffs along the shore, fly the sea birds – gulls, kittiwakes, terns, fulmars, and murres. Diving beneath the sea for its food is a king eider duck, sharing the underwater domain with Arctic char and Arctic cod. In the shallows the huge walrus grubs on the bottom for clams and molluscs, somewhat prosaic fare for such a mighty mammal of the sea.

80

Arctic Terns

Polar Bear

Beluga Whales

Polar Cod

Crustacean

Herring

Fox Den Arctic Fox Cubs Willow Ptarmigan Ground Squirrel Arctic Poppies Lesser Fritillary Arctic Bee

Summer visitors and winter residents— an ever-changing panorama

In winter the Arctic coast is a near-empty land of ice and snow. In their dens the barren ground grizzlies sleep quietly, and ground squirrels barely breathe in hibernation. Many of the great herds of caribou have retreated into the sub-Arctic northern forest, leaving behind only scattered bands to winter on the tundra. Beneath the snow cover lemmings

Barren Ground Grizzly Bear Ground Squirrel Barren Ground Caribou Rock Ptarmigan

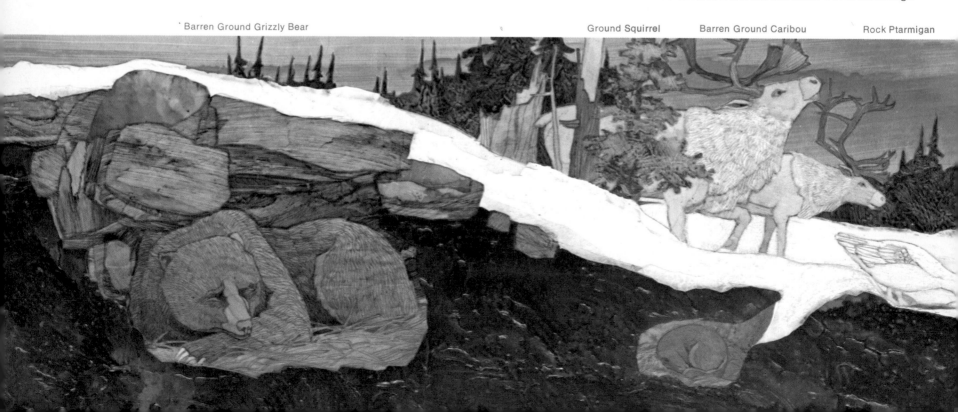

Barren Ground Caribou   Arctic Hare   Wolf   Male Pintail   Female Pintail   Barren Ground Caribou

scamper about in their tunnels; beneath the thick ice cover on the larger lakes, Arctic char swim and feed. Near the edge-of-trees the wily wolverine hunts Arctic hares; ptarmigan feed in flocks, preyed upon by the falcon in its white phase. In summer all this changes; the snow disappears, the ice on the lakes melts, flowers bloom and insects buzz,

pintails swim gracefully in ponds, and herds of caribou invade the tundra once more to feed and drop their calves. Everywhere there is life and movement and sound as bears and ground squirrels awake, hares flee for their lives from the Arctic wolf, and thousands of migrating birds fill the air with their cries. *Panorama continued overleaf.*

Wolverine   Arctic Hare   Arctic Char   Wolf   Falcon   Rock Ptarmigan

Arctic Crocus   Arctic Wolf   Lemming   Musk Oxen   Lichen   Lemming   Arctic Cotton Grass

Under the stimulus of twenty-four hour sunlight, flora buds, blooms and withers with startling rapidity. Arctic crocus and white tufts of cotton grass bob in the breeze. Among the grasses and flowers, lemmings and ground squirrels search for food, and become food, for prowling wolves and foxes. Herds of musk ox prowl placidly across their home valleys while the young grow big and fat on the combination of fresh fodder and mother's milk. Great flocks of snow geese feed in the marshes and lay their eggs in down-lined nests on the gravel ridges. Through the long day of the short summer, the mean daily temperature on the Arctic coast remains uniform at about forty degrees (compared to sixty-eight degrees at Winnipeg and seventy-one degrees at Montreal) but the mid-day temperature can climb as high as sixty-five to seventy

Lemming   Arctic Fox   Female Polar Bear and Cub   Snowy Owl

Snow Geese

degrees at some locations, and has been known to reach a high of eighty. All this is in violent contrast to the winter months when great stretches of the Arctic coast appear to be snow and ice-covered wasteland. Most of the birds have gone; insects have disappeared; flora is almost all buried under hard-packed snow. But life goes on through the long, dark winter; lemmings scuttle about in tunnels under the snow, polar bears prowl inland looking for food, followed in turn by hungry foxes and ravens which share the find. The snowy owl wings his silent way over the snow, and the long, eerie howl of the wolf echoes across the snow-covered valleys as he and his family group hunt caribou, and, when driven by a need to fill their hungry bellies, will attack the powerfully-built musk ox. In winter, the Arctic coast is a land of feast or famine.

Wolf Pack

Musk Oxen

Raven

Polar Bears

Arctic Fox

Snow

Ringed Seal Pup in Den

Ringed Seals

Snow

Breathing Holes

Ice

Ringed Seals

Mother Seal

Ice

The ringed seal – a mammal of the northern sea

Without seals there could never have arisen the coastal Eskimo hunting culture. Seals provided the Arctic hunter with almost everything he needed—skins for clothing and summer shelter, fat as food and as oil for the lamps, flesh for food. Four main types of seals are to be found—the rare bladder-nose seal; the harp seal of the southern waters; the solitary square-flipper, or bearded seal, and the ringed

Sabine's Gulls

Glaucous Gulls

Stranded Ice Floe

Eskimo in Kayak

Ringed Seals

Phalaropes

Ringed Seals

Arctic Char

seal, or jar. The seal must have air to breathe and comes to the surface often in order to get air. In the fall, the seal pushes up the rubbery sea ice with its head to form a number of shallow domes filled with air. Through winter the seal returns to these domes to breathe, keeping each opening clear of new-forming ice. In the spring the females enlarge one or more of the holes, usually one beneath a large snowdrift in the lee of rafted ice. The seal pups are born in a cave cleared under the snow. Young seals are the favourite food of prowling foxes and bears who break in the cave tops to get at them before they can escape down the breathing hole to the safety of the sea. By mid-April the seals scramble onto the ice surface through the breathing holes, to bask in the warm spring sun.

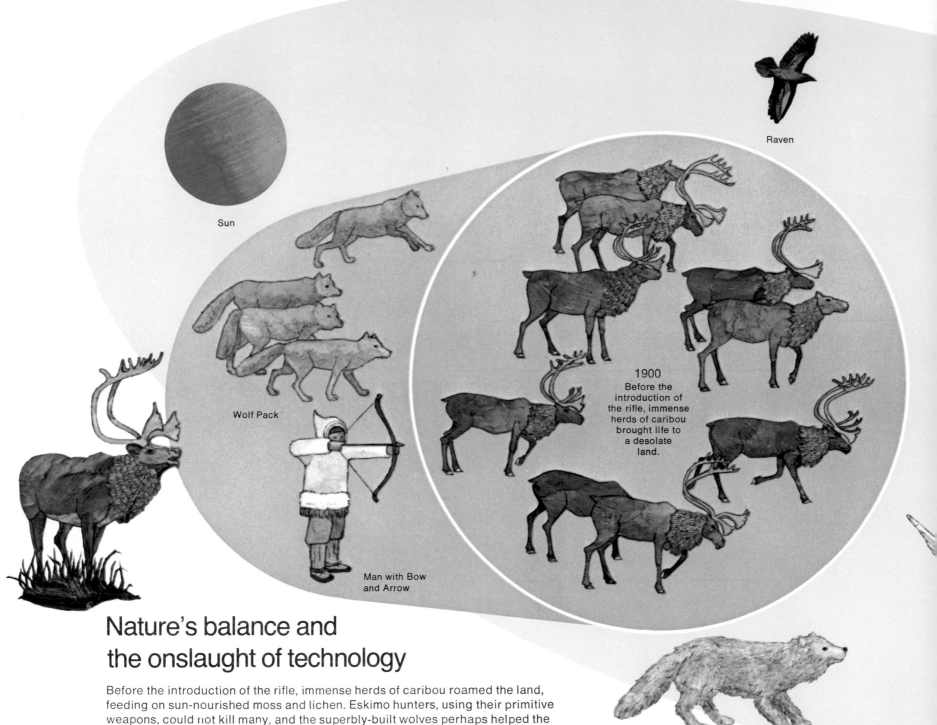

Sun

Raven

Wolf Pack

Man with Bow
and Arrow

1900
Before the
introduction of
the rifle, immense
herds of caribou
brought life to
a desolate
land.

Arctic Fox

Nature's balance and
the onslaught of technology

Before the introduction of the rifle, immense herds of caribou roamed the land,
feeding on sun-nourished moss and lichen. Eskimo hunters, using their primitive
weapons, could not kill many, and the superbly-built wolves perhaps helped the
caribou by weeding out the weakest of the species. Scavenging on leftover kills
came the raven, the Arctic fox, the gull and the aloof barren-ground grizzly.
Modern-day enemies of the caribou include track vehicles, which disturb the tundra, fire and aircraft which terrify and cause stampedes, and although there are
fewer of the fearsome wolves, man now wields a deadly accurate rifle.

Raven

Aircraft

Fire

Tracked Vehicles

Man with Rifle

Wolves

1965
The handsome caribou, an important
link in the food chain of the Arctic,
has been depleted over a sixty-five year
period to one-tenth its former population.
Range-destroying fire, and poor calf
crops due to bad weather have been
contributing factors, but the
excessive kills caused by the
rifle have been most to blame.

Gulls

Grizzly

A scavenging raven feeds hungrily on caribou meat.

PART FOUR / ANIMAL LIFE

9 THE AIR ABOVE

All winter the land and frozen water surface of the Arctic is a white wilderness; mile after mile it stretches away endlessly to the distant horizon, thousands upon thousands of acres of treeless, snow-covered soil and rock and ice, a vista of white broken only by the dark rock hilltops or the shiny blue-green of the wind-blasted ice along the northern shores of the lakes. Across the face of this bare, and often bitter, land the winter wind shrieks in wild abandon, whipping up the snow to blot out the sun and the sky until the Arctic world is shrunk to a few square feet within the swirling walls of formless white. On quiet days the wind rustles gently over the snow; the land lies still and serene, the air filled with millions of dancing, twinkling diamonds of ice that reflect the red, red rays of the three suns hanging low on the horizon to the south.

In mid-winter the tundra seems devoid of life; rarely is there any movement other than that of snow granules snaking their sinuous, shifting lines across the hard packed snow. The winter tundra has its herds of caribou, sometimes hundreds of them together; it has its groups of musk ox, grazing in their sheltered valleys; it has its wolves and foxes and hares, but so vast is this far north land that it swallows them all; it engulfs them, singly or in their hundreds so that the tundra is like an immense white desert, a harsh and often cruel land, merciless to the unwary, granting life only grudgingly, quick to drive out or destroy any who fail to adhere to its terms for survival.

Empty the land seems, and especially does it seem empty of birds—no cheeps or song, no graceful forms flitting across the blue of the sky. And why should this not be so? This Arctic land has destroyed or driven out far mightier forms of life than the fragile birds; it destroyed the mighty mammoth, it forced the huge barren ground grizzly to endure a life pattern of winter sleep each year, it imposed upon the great herds of mainland caribou a life of constant movement in which most must head south for the shelter of the trees each autumn. Indeed, it would seem strange if the delicate birds did not go south for the winter, as most of them do. Most of them, but not all; for so adaptable is life on planet earth that it has developed within a few species of birds special qualities that enable them to live year round, to reproduce and multiply in a land completely dominated by cold. And in one bird it has developed a body and a spirit so tough and unyielding that it makes no visible concession to cold; winter and summer the coal-black, bare-footed raven sneers contemptuously at its Arctic environment as if by strength of will alone it has met and mastered the worst conditions that can come its way.

The raven is a bird of the north, big, tough, strong, afraid of nothing, and in possession of an uncanny ability to "home" on any form of food from extremely long distances away. Even in mid-winter, when deep cold renders any odour almost negligible, the raven can sense a meal from afar. To see three or four ravens winging their way above the frozen tundra with a definite sense of purpose and direction to their flight, is to know that a herd of caribou with its attendant wolves can be found in that direction, that before long the ravens will be picking at a carcass lying bloody and still on the snow. To travel on the sea ice off the high, rocky cliffs of east Baffin Island and encounter ravens heading toward the edge of the land-fast floe some three to four miles out from shore is to know that a polar bear has killed a seal, and is now enjoying a meal of fresh fat and meat that it will soon have to share with the croaking birds winging their way unerringly toward the food that is far out of their sight.

Just how the raven senses meat over distant horizons is not known; nor is it known how the raven is able to exist on the Arctic coast year round without seeming to make any concessions to the cold and bitter winter weather. But live on the Arctic coast it does, coal-black the year round, feet and legs bare of any protecting feathers, seemingly completely indifferent to wind and cold, and equally indifferent to the threat of death or injury under the claws and jaws of the mammals upon whose fresh kills it so often feeds. I do not know if ravens tease polar bears or wolves, but I suspect they do. I do know they tease dogs unmercifully, often acting in concert in order to get at desired food. At an Eskimo camp on north Baffin Island I watched as three ravens sat on the snow-covered sea ice about ten feet from a big sled dog who was gnawing on a piece of frozen seal meat. The dog was untethered but the ravens, positioned in a circle about him, were not the least bit afraid. After a few moments one of the ravens hopped in toward the dog and immediately the dog stopped gnawing and growled deep in his throat. A second raven hopped in closer; with a rush the dog came to his feet and dashed at the first raven which merely hopped back, with considerable dignity, barely keeping clear of the dog's jaws. The second and third ravens dashed for the piece of meat lying unguarded on the snow but before they could reach it the dog had turned on them to send them into squawking flight.

The dog settled down to eat; in a few minutes the ravens again took up their positions on the snow; again one of them hopped in close. The dog's head came up and a low growl rumbled in his throat. Once again the second raven hopped in close; the dog leaped up, charged first at one raven and then turned to charge back at the other. But the second charge led him too far from the piece of meat; the first raven hopped in with almost contemptuous slowness to pick up the meat and rise majestically into the air. All three ravens flew along the beach, enticing the baffled dog to follow them, before sweeping into the sky to disappear around a distant point where they could enjoy their stolen meal in squabbling peace.

Of the many birds found in the Arctic there are only eight that spend their lives in the country north of the tree line—the raven, the snowy owl, the gyrfalcon, the willow and the rock ptarmigan, and three members of the auk family, the black guillemot, the thick-billed murre, and the dovekie. All other birds are migratory, coming to the Arctic each spring and summer to nest and raise their young, but flying south as soon as the first touch of winter sweeps over the land. Even the snow bunting, which is a northern bird and often re-appears on the tundra late in winter long before any sign of spring melt, abandons the Arctic in mid-winter for the somewhat less rigorous climate of southern Canada where it can be seen feeding in large flocks along the roadsides and in the farm fields.

The true Arctic birds have made adaptations to the cold, and to the fluctuating temperatures, of their far north homeland in much the same way as the Arctic mammals. For the birds, feathers perform their basic flight function but they also serve as excellent insulation, corresponding to the fur of the mammal. Feathers of Arctic birds are generally a little longer than those of related birds to the south and, in most species, plumage changes in density with the season—more feathers in winter than in summer for extra warmth. Snowy owls and ptarmigan grow

The red-throated loon builds his nest in a heap of moss or other vegetation, very close to the water's edge in marshy areas.

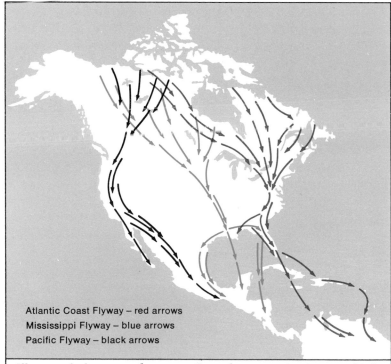

Atlantic Coast Flyway – red arrows
Mississippi Flyway – blue arrows
Pacific Flyway – black arrows

Illustrated above are the routes flown by many Arctic coast birds on their way south after summering in the northern regions.

Sparrow (northern)

Sparrow (southern)

Willow Ptarmigan (winter)

Willow Ptarmigan
(summer)

Willow Ptarmigan
Hiding in snow bank

Larger than his southern counterparts, the sparrow is better able to withstand the cold; willow ptarmigan change colour with the seasons.

feathers on their legs as well as on their bodies; in winter ptarmigan even grow a thick covering of feathers on both feet right up to the claws, giving them a somewhat comical appearance as they strut over the hard-packed snow. At the start of an Arctic storm ptarmigan will plunge into the nearest bank of softer snow where they will remain snug and safe from the violent winds above.

Although the raven is the most unusual, the ptarmigan is the most truly Arctic bird. Two species are found north of the tree line—the willow ptarmigan and the rock. The willow ptarmigan is the larger; its habitat is the tundra and upland valleys of the mainland Arctic coast and the lower Arctic islands. The rock ptarmigan has a more extensive range over the tundra biome; it is found everywhere from lower Hudson Bay in the south to northern Ellesmere Island in the far north, both summer and winter, although many of the far north flocks migrate to the southern edges of the tundra during the winter, occasionally travelling as far south as James Bay.

The ptarmigan belongs in the *Tetraonidae* family, fowl-like birds widely represented all across the northern hemisphere. It is a relative of the grouse but a little larger than its cousin to the south, thus taking advantage of the general, but not infallible rule, that larger size enables a bird, or a mammal, to better withstand cold—the larger the body surface is in proportion to the bulk, the less is the amount of heat that will be lost through the body surface. The matter of large size is also an advantage

to birds during the Arctic winter when food is in much shorter supply. A small bird has more surface per volume of heat producing tissue than a large bird and therefore it needs more food per unit of body weight. Of all species of birds that live in the Arctic for at least a portion of each year about sixty per cent are pigeon size or larger, compared to only thirty per cent of all birds in southern Ontario.

In summer the rock ptarmigan has a brownish-grey speckled plumage (male) or a barred, black and white plumage (female), except for the wings which are white. In winter both sexes have an all-white plumage except for an eye bar of black, and black tail feathers with white tips, of which only the white tips show unless the bird is in flight. The all-white covering is an excellent camouflage; ptarmigan will freeze if danger threatens so as to be practically invisible against the white snow. The black, or white, or black and white pattern of coloration is standard among Arctic birds; the tundra is a hard land, not prone to encourage the development of non-essential frills of any kind. Arctic birds have few colours and when they do such colour is confined to the naked areas of the head and feet.

Arctic birds share with Arctic mammals the ability to maintain a double standard of internal body temperature, especially the sea birds that spend the greater part of their time, winter and summer, swimming on or in the icy water of the sea, or standing for long periods on the ice itself. Extra body fat, an undercoat of down plus fluffy, oily feathers keep the body and the wings of

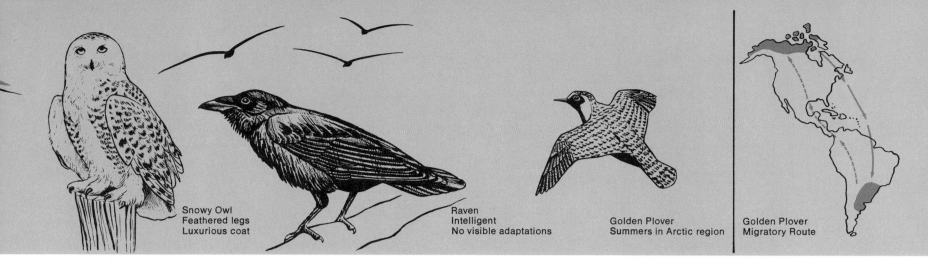

The golden plover is a migratory bird, while the snowy owl and the raven have adapted well to a year-round life in the cold regions.

Snowy Owl
Feathered legs
Luxurious coat

Raven
Intelligent
No visible adaptations

Golden Plover
Summers in Arctic region

Golden Plover
Migratory Route

the guillemot warm and dry as it explores for food far down in the water beneath the sea ice cover. But its legs and feet have no such protection. Similarly the gull that stands for hours on a pinnacle of ice waiting and watching for food, has bare feet in direct contact with the ice. Experiments in Alaska have shown that the temperature within the feet of a gull can be near 32 degrees Fahrenheit, just above the freezing point and about 70 degrees cooler than the rest of the body. Along with this colder temperature in the legs, the gulls seem able to increase the circulation of the blood to the legs and feet without any rise in temperature taking place. Such birds, extremely tolerant of cold, are able to move about and function well at low temperatures that would completely immobilize a bird accustomed only to the temperatures of the temperate zone.

Despite the phenomenal ability of the gull to stand for long periods on bare ice, it, like most of the birds that come to the Arctic, is a great coward, or it is blessed with an extraordinary amount of common sense, or it reacts to stimuli implanted within its being many thousands of years ago. Most birds found on the Arctic coast in summer don't wait around for the winter weather; long before the cold turns the Arctic into a land of ice and snow, they head off south, flying fast and far, over and around almost all barriers of mountains, seas and deserts. For most Arctic birds their adaptation to cold has been to flee, to head west, east and south away from the Arctic coast in a great mass movement that we call migration.

In summer the tundra is home to hawks, falcons, jaegers, owls, all of which prey upon the smaller birds, ptarmigan, plovers, turnstones, curlews, sandpipers, phalaropes, larks, sparrows, longspur, and the ubiquitous snow bunting. In certain areas sandhill cranes nest and feed; in the marshy regions loons, swans and ducks fight for territory, nest and raise their young before gathering in huge flocks to fly south again. Year after year the birds return to the same nesting grounds, usually arriving within a few days of a certain time in the late spring. Despite their tremendous ability to navigate, the birds are poor weather prophets. Regardless of the climatic conditions at the nesting site the birds always arrive at their allotted time to begin the nesting. In 1953 summer on north Baffin Island was very late in arriving; June was a month of extreme cold and violent storms. At the snow geese nesting grounds on Bylot Island geese sat on eggs in nests on the ground, buried up to their necks in new snow, with long drifts extending downwind from their bodies.

On the tundra the small birds feed on the millions of insects that fill the air during the summer months. Others feed on the seeds of the grasses, on the berries of the bushes. The predators feed on eggs, on the smaller birds, and on the lemmings and mice that scamper about the tundra biome "forest." All through the twenty-four hours of daylight each summer day the birds are on the nests or on the move, full of energy and vitality, as if conscious of the fact that their time on the Arctic coast is short —urgency is the order of the day, there is no time to lose. So well developed is this sense of limited time that some species go through the annual courtship stage on the long flight north, arriving at the breeding ground ready to nest immediately. Nesting must be a success the first time; failure means a wait until next year to try again. The eggs are laid, the young are born and grow to youth in a non-stop cycle of activity, allowing no time for any post-breeding loaf period; often the birds moult gradually while on the move or they postpone this process until after their arrival on the southern wintering grounds.

On the treeless tundra all species of birds nest on the ground, either on the gravel ridges as do the snow geese, within the hummocks of patterned ground as do most of the small birds, or on the grassy hummocks of the swamps as do the loons. Often species of birds, or certain birds and mammals, will establish a symbiotic relationship at the nesting grounds to help ensure their survival. On the wide gravel hills of southern Bylot Island colonies of snow geese nest each year, building their foot-diameter, down-lined nests in slight hollows in the gravel. A single colony will extend over some three or four acres, the flat, stony ground covered with nesting hollows in which the female lays anywhere from half a dozen to a dozen and more chicken-size eggs. Sometimes the colony will have one or more brood nests in which surplus eggs are laid and abandoned; it is not unusual to find such nests full to overflowing with two or three dozen unattended eggs, often so many that the ground around is covered as well. Many of the snow geese colony sites will have a small hill within the area, on which a snowy owl will nest. The owls do not harm the geese or their eggs; they serve as sentinels, warning of the approach of foxes, driving away foxes by their swooping attacks and thus helping both themselves and the geese.

Without the advantage of nesting in trees away from ground predators, Arctic birds have had to develop other means of ensuring their continued survival. Many species have exceptionally well-developed distraction techniques by which either male or female flutters along the ground dragging a wing as if injured, thereby distracting the fox or the wolf away from the nest and the young. The generally dun-coloured ground birds fit well into the background of grass and moss among which they build their nests; the ptarmigan in its summer coat is almost as invisible as it is in its winter white. Jaegers and terns use a dive bomb technique to drive away foxes and wolves, and humans as well, swooping down from heights of fifty to seventy-five feet in near vertical dives at the bottom of which they often hit the mammals a blow with a wing before streaking back up into the sky for another swoop. The birds also use such dives as a hunting technique; often they will follow foxes, wolves, bears, even caribou walking over the tundra, watching for the small birds startled by the passage of the animal.

Although the tundra is home for thousands of summer land birds, the biggest groups contain the sea birds that nest on the bird cliffs found all through the eastern Arctic coast region. Gulls, fulmars, kittiwakes, murres all nest in huge colonies at specific locations to which they return year after year. Every Eskimo hunter knows the locations of the bird nesting cliffs in his area and, in the days of old, would travel there with his family in the early summer to eat the eggs and the young birds as a welcome change to his winter diet of meat and fish. Digges Island, at the western entrance to Hudson Strait, is the site of huge murre nesting colonies; fulmars nest at cliffs all along the east coast fiords of Baffin, Devon and Ellesmere Islands; the rugged cliffs of Pelly and Committee Bays on the north coasts have famous gull cliffs, both on the sea coast and on the steep cliffs of the inland hills.

One of the oddities of the Arctic is a little bird, a summer dweller which comes to the Arctic each year to nest and raise its young before heading south for the winter. The bird is the phalarope, a small water species related to the sandpiper. The phalarope looks much like any other shore bird but the superficial resemblance is deceiving. In the bird world it is almost always the male that is the bright-coloured member of the family. Not the phalarope—the female is bright-coloured while the male is dull. In the bird world the male is always the first to arrive at the breeding ground, to select the nest site and then remain with the female while she lays the eggs and raises the young. Not so the phalarope—the female arrives first at the nesting area and picks out the site. She lays the eggs but it is the male bird that sits and hatches them while the female defends the home. In the phalarope, at some time in the distant past, chance mutation seems to have caused certain sexual characteristics to become reversed and, as a result, the phalarope ended up as a freak in the bird world.

BIRDS OF THE NORTHERN SKIES

In summer the Arctic coast plays host to thousands upon thousands of birds, most of which, like the long-tailed jaeger in the picture above, have flown hundreds of miles along ancient migration routes. Some birds arrive from the south, like the Arctic tern which has come all the way from Antarctica. Other birds come from southeast and southwest— the yellow-billed loon winters on the Pacific coast; Canadian fulmars winter in the North Atlantic. Wheeling and crying over land and sea the birds bring visible and audible life to every nook and cranny of our far northland.

Techniques for survival

Having to nest on the ground robs most birds of the protection from predators afforded by nests in trees. Different protection techniques are used by different species of birds. Ptarmigan depend on camouflage in winter and summer. Almost invisible in winter white or summer brown, ptarmigan will freeze when danger threatens, exploding into violent flight only if directly threatened. Small birds build their tiny nests under low bushes, or beneath overhanging clumps of hummocky, frozen ground. Geese and swans remain white all summer and nest in plain sight, relying on size, fighting ability and distraction techniques to ensure their continued survival. Loons nest on dry hummocks in the middle of swampy areas; hawks build their nests on ledges of the rocky cliffs. At the bird cliffs or the steep rock shores of many Arctic islands, sea birds such as gulls, kittiwakes, terns, fulmars, nest high on the rocky ledges safe from all but predatory birds, and hunting man. For three months the birds are everywhere on the land; then, almost overnight, they are gone on the long migration routes to their summer homes.

The male rock ptarmigan is shown at upper left, complete with protective feathers covering his legs and feet. Crouching immobile in her summer nest, the female willow ptarmigan, left, is well camouflaged.

The four eggs shown below belong to
the tiny tree sparrow, a summer
visitor to the Arctic. The nest is
almost invisible in the dense under-
brush, and the young are guarded and
fed (right) by an adult sparrow who
depends on her summer camouflage
for protection against predators.

The newly-hatched cygnet sitting in a
nest safely hidden by the long grass,
(above) will mature in a few years into
a beautiful whistling swan. Skins of
these summer visitors were once traded
as furs, but are now protected by law.

A wary young gyrfalcon (pictured overleaf) sits safely in his nest on the
cliffside high above the Kazan River.

10 FAUNAL ADAPTATION TO THE COLD

The Arctic coast region is a land area under the influence of ice, within which all life must adapt to the fact of extreme cold. But the basic adjustment of the life forms is not so much to the cold itself as it is to the very wide fluctuations in temperature through the yearly cycle of heat and cold. As a minimum requirement all tundra fauna, as well as flora, must be able to exist at a temperature of 60° above zero as well as at a temperature of 60° below, a range of 120 degrees.

Insects have had no difficulty in adjusting to the variations of climate within the Arctic, a fact that can be verified by anyone who has suffered under the clouds of millions upon millions of mosquitoes that swarm over the tundra during the summer months. In 1743, the Chief Factor of the recently completed Fort Prince of Wales on the west coast of Hudson Bay, observed that "Mosquitoes bite with their sharp bill in such a manner that shall have our heads swelled as big as a tilterkin [a large cask]; as to a man's not seeing a mark he fires at for them is nothing, . . . you may very well sweep a bushel off one man's head; they have been so thick we have been obliged to shovel them away before we could get in at the doors!" In the years since that time mosquitoes haven't lessened in numbers at all.

But why should insects be bothered by the minor inconvenience of cold? Insects have existed on earth in approximately the same numbers as they are today for the past 300 million years during which time they have had plenty of time to work out adjustments that enable them to live under almost any conditions known on planet earth. Certain insects live in hot springs where the temperature of the water reaches 120 degrees Fahrenheit; others have been frozen solid and lived to breed and multiply; some species survive in laboratories in an almost total vacuum. Insects live in deep, underground caves; others can exist in the air at altitudes of 20,000 feet. The young of the brine fly live in almost pure salt; petroleum flies spend their immature stages in pools of crude oil; a grain weevil can live for hours in an atmosphere of pure carbon dioxide. On the bleak Antarctic continent, although there are no truly land mammals or birds, over forty kinds of insects live and thrive.

To the insects the cold and fluctuating temperature of the Arctic coast region must have seemed a rather minor problem to which they adjusted with ease. Bees, beetles, moths and butterflies live as far north as flowering plants grow, decreasing only in variety of species and in numbers of certain species. Mosquitoes live wherever there are warm-blooded animals like the caribou and musk ox, the Arctic hare and the ground squirrel, from which they can draw blood. Blowfly larvae breed wherever there are carcasses of lemmings and mice to serve as their hosts; earthworms, spiders, mites, midges, flies find food and protection in the burrows and nests of these Arctic rodents. No Arctic land surface seems too poor or too cold to support some insect life; tiny Meighen Island in the high Arctic, described by Stefansson as "the most nearly barren land that I have ever seen," supports at least two arthropods that find sustenance from seventeen types of plant life, and from the scattered droppings of a few visiting birds and the odd, wandering caribou.

The land mammals and birds of the tundra biome have not been able to duplicate the extremes of adaptation of the flora and the insects; they found other means to protect their warm bodies in order to ensure continued survival and reproduction of their own kind. Most birds take advantage of their flight facility to leave the Arctic coast altogether during the cold period, returning only when the weather has warmed up again. Some mammals enter a state of dormancy or hibernation, a pale imitation of the hibernation of the flora, in which they exist for at least a part of the long, cold winter period. Other mammals, and a few of the birds, have insulated covers for their bodies, either as fur or feathers, that change density with the season allowing them to exist in reasonable comfort at sixty below or sixty above and it is becoming increasingly evident that all Arctic mammals and birds have developed controls that regulate metabolism and circulation so as to cope with excess heat as well as excess cold.

All birds and mammals of the tundra are warm blooded, deriving their body heat from energy produced from the foods they eat. The colder the outside air temperature, the more food they require to maintain body heat. The temperature at which man, a warm-blooded mammal without fur covering of any kind, starts to lose heat is quite high, about 80 degrees Fahrenheit. In order to halt this loss, or slow it down, some form of

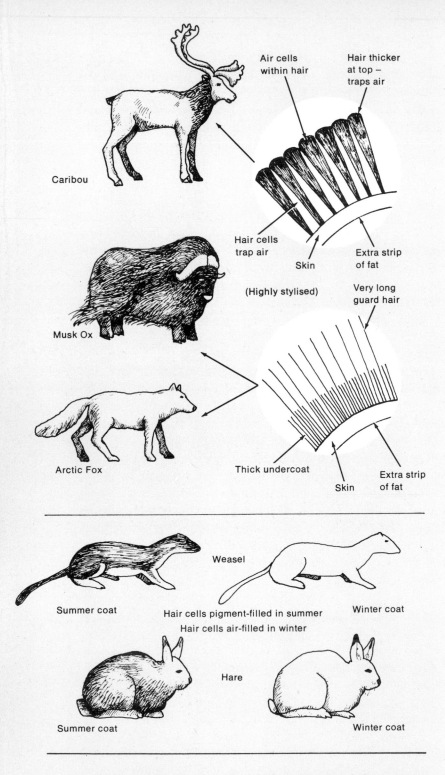

Labels in figure:

Caribou

Air cells within hair

Hair thicker at top — traps air

Hair cells trap air

Skin

Extra strip of fat

(Highly stylised)

Musk Ox

Very long guard hair

Arctic Fox

Thick undercoat

Skin

Extra strip of fat

Weasel

Summer coat

Hair cells pigment-filled in summer
Hair cells air-filled in winter

Winter coat

Hare

Summer coat

Winter coat

Survival of animal life in a generally harsh Arctic environment necessitates several adaptive techniques, such as seasonal changes in the extent, type and coloration of the Arctic mammal's fur coat.

outer covering becomes a necessity and the greater the degree of cold the heavier the covering that will be required. Thus, all warm-blooded mammals of the Arctic coast have developed thick coats of fur to trap the heat produced by eating large quantities of food. Most mammals reinforce this fur insulation by taking shelter for at least part of the time, in burrows in the ground, in burrows under the snow, or in snow caves dug into the deep drifts that form in the lee of the hills and ice hummocks.

The type, extent and coloration of the fur on the Arctic mammals varies considerably. Probably the best protected is the Arctic fox which has a fur coat consisting of long guard hairs over a short underwool. So efficient is the protection of his luxuriant winter coat, the fox has no need to move about to create warmth until the outside temperature falls below minus forty degrees. The huge musk ox is another example of this double type of coat; it has a thick undercoat of wool up through which grows a mat of very long guard hairs, so long they trail on the ground by the late winter, providing extra protection to the legs and feet. The pelage of the caribou is of a different type; it is a single fur covering of hair that grows anew each season, getting progressively longer all through the cold months of fall and winter before being shed in the early summer. Each hair of the caribou fur is full of tiny air cells within the hair stem, and each is thicker at the tip than it is at the base, thus trapping dead air within the fur coat, increasing greatly the insulation value without any increase in the weight.

Many Arctic mammals change the colour of their fur to white, or off-white, in the winter months; the fox, the weasel, the hare of the mainland and lower islands, all change from a generally brownish summer colour to a winter coat of almost solid white. This serves as a protective device against their predators, but it also serves an insulation function as well, for the cells within the hair that are filled with pigment in the summer are filled with air in the winter. The polar bear remains white, or off-white, the year round; the musk ox retains its brown colour. Caribou of the mainland seem to have more white hair in winter than they do in summer, although this may be a result of the hair being longer; the polar caribou of the high Arctic islands have considerably more white hair in their fur than do their cousins on the islands and mainland to the south.

Insulation about the body of the mammals also takes the form of an invisible layer of fat immediately beneath the skin. This is less well developed in the land mammals than in the sea mammals and probably serves more as storage of tissue to produce extra heat during the winter months. The fat is produced from the carbohydrates in the food eaten during the relatively warm days of summer and fall. The long, thick strips of fat that form along the back of the caribou are a favourite delicacy of the Arctic coast Eskimo hunters.

Although it is not an all-encompassing principle, Arctic mammals are often larger than their counterparts to the south; the larger an object, the more slowly it tends to lose heat which is a definite advantage in the tundra biome. Along with larger size, Arctic mammals have much smaller appendages; ears, noses, tails are almost always stubby with less surface to radiate away body heat. Mammals like the fox, the wolf and the husky dog can fluff out the fur around their bodies to entrap more air and add, at least temporarily, to their warmth. They can also modify their basic shape so as to make it more compact and reduce the amount of surface radiating heat to the outer air. Anyone who has seen an Eskimo dog curled up into a tight ball with nose tucked under curled-up tail, feet and legs hinged beneath the ball of the body, tiny ears pressed flat into the heavy fur of the head and all fur fluffed up while he sleeps soundly in the open, oblivious to the thirty below temperature and the howling wind, will have seen the near ultimate of inter-acting forces designed for the conservation of body heat in the cold.

The least understood of all the factors that enable Arctic mammals to withstand great cold and extreme fluctuations of temperature are the internal processes which act so as to conserve or dissipate heat. Dissipation of excess heat is almost as important as the retention of heat, especially to animals like the caribou which may be grazing peacefully one minute and in full flight over the tundra the next. Thinner fur on the belly area, ears, legs and tail serve, along with the standard panting tongue, as means of getting rid of excess heat. In addition, many Arctic mammals can withstand temperatures as much as fifty degrees higher than those tolerated by some desert mammals, their metabolic processes geared to respond to excess of heat through the same set of controls that acts to cope with excess cold. Caribou, dogs and wolves, as well as birds, have a double standard

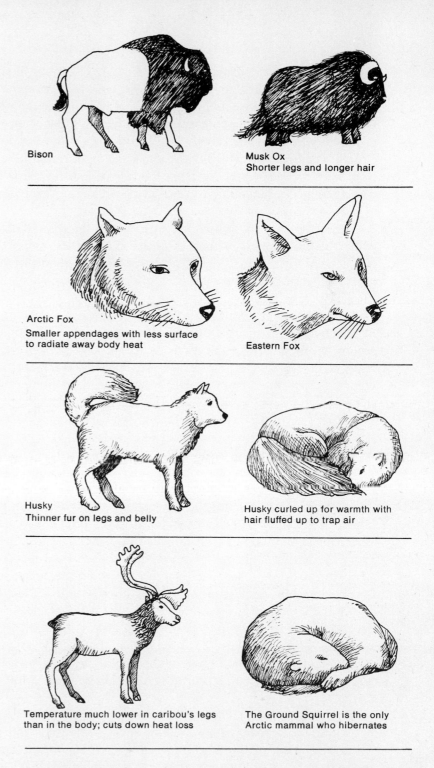

Bison

Musk Ox
Shorter legs and longer hair

Arctic Fox
Smaller appendages with less surface
to radiate away body heat

Eastern Fox

Husky
Thinner fur on legs and belly

Husky curled up for warmth with
hair fluffed up to trap air

Temperature much lower in caribou's legs
than in the body; cuts down heat loss

The Ground Squirrel is the only
Arctic mammal who hibernates

The metabolic processes of Arctic mammals are geared to respond to excesses of heat or cold, in order to be able to withstand an extreme temperature fluctuation from sixty below to sixty above.

of body temperature; in their legs temperature is kept as much as fifty degrees lower than in their bodies, cutting down on the heat loss through these extremities. This temperature differential is accomplished by means of a simple heat-exchange mechanism in the body; arteries carrying warm blood toward the legs are closely bunched and twined with veins carrying the cold blood from the legs back to the heart; in this way the warm blood is cooled and the cold blood is warmed in a never-ending exchange of heat and cold.

Strangely enough, although it would seem that hibernation would be the simplest method by which the smaller mammals could avoid the excess cold and the restricted food supply of the long winter period in the Arctic, only one mammal actually hibernates—the little Arctic ground squirrel. True hibernation, as opposed to long periods of otherwise normal sleep accompanied by periods of wakening and movement, is a rare thing among all mammals of the earth. What physiological process triggers hibernation is not yet known, except that the onset coincides with the advent of cold weather in the autumn and the resulting disappearance of the food supply. It is possible that the shortening of the daylight hours may be what triggers hibernation. Many northern mammals can be induced to vary normal reproduction cycles when subjected to periods of artificial light that do not correspond to the actual length of the day; normal spring activity of the pituitary and sex glands can be slowed down by artificially keeping the "day" short as if it were still midwinter or the mammals can be induced to reproduce in winter under the stimulus of an artificial, very long day.

When the ground squirrel hibernates for the winter its body temperature drops to only a few degrees above the freezing mark and its normally rapid breathing slows down until it is difficult to tell if the animal is breathing or not. Its heart beats at the very slow rate of five to ten beats per minute as opposed to a normal two to four hundred. Curled up in a tight ball in its snug burrow under the sod and snow, a hibernating ground squirrel is almost dead; it can be picked up and put down again without a stir.

Mice, lemmings, shrews, all small mammals of the tundra, are content to spend only a small part of the winter in a state of dormancy; most of the time they scamper about within their interlocking tunnels under the frozen ground and under the snow, foraging for frozen green vegetation or feeding on stored seeds and roots, or in the case of the shrew, on stored insects. The weasel, the hare, the fox and the wolf roam the tundra all winter. The barren ground grizzly enters a period of long winter sleep in its tundra den but this is not considered to be true hibernation. The polar bear does not hibernate, although the female bear will den up in a huge snow cave to await the birth of her cubs early in the spring. The male bear roams the ice of the Arctic seas so long as he is able to find food for his stomach; when food is scarce in mid-winter he digs a den in a snowbank and goes to sleep for a few days, or a few weeks, existing on body fat and stored energy in his tissues. Eskimo hunters fear few Arctic mammals but they have a healthy respect for the polar bear, and they are especially cautious when approaching a hungry male just out from a long sleep.

Although research is not yet sufficiently well developed to provide a complete picture of exactly how each Arctic mammal has adapted to the cold and fluctuating temperature regime of the tundra biome, present studies indicate that a close interrelationship between various physiological, morphological and behavioral factors exists within each mammal. These can be best illustrated in a study of the musk ox, the largest of the Arctic coast strictly land mammals, and the one best adjusted to a year round existence on the open tundra.

The musk ox stands up to five feet in height at the shoulder and can weigh as much as seven to eight hundred pounds. Being so large it requires large quantities of food, both summer and winter, for it roams a restricted range at all seasons of the year. The musk ox is herbivorous, preferring certain foods like willow and grasses, but it will eat anything that grows on the tundra, an important survival factor for such a large animal in a cold land where food is often sparse and annual production of all vegetation is low. Because the musk ox must move about and find food through the very long dark period of winter as well as the correspondingly bright period of spring and early summer when glare from the snow cover is extreme, it has eyes that adapt well to either condition. From the plants it finds and eats it derives energy for growth and, in addition, it seems able to store energy within certain organs of its body. During the summer months, when the vegetation is plentiful, the weight of its liver increases quite considerably, suggesting that food stored in this organ

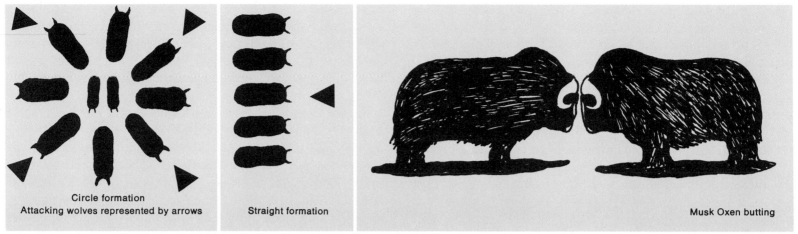

Circle formation
Attacking wolves represented by arrows

Straight formation

Musk Oxen butting

Defence positions taken by musk oxen are in the shape of a circle or a straight line, protecting the females and the young. When aroused by sensed danger, two huge bulls will often charge each other, and after the tremendous crash, back off to resume grazing.

during the summer and early fall may be an important source of energy during the lean months of winter. The musk ox produces within its rumen the various B vitamins, therefore these need not be a part of the food it eats. Biologists believe that the musk ox is able to synthesize protein from the nitrogen contained in the food it eats, which is especially helpful when the protein levels in the food are low as they must be in the dry grasses eaten during the winter months. They believe also that the musk ox is able to recycle nitrogen within its body instead of discharging it in the urine. Musk ox dung changes form from winter to summer—in summer it is soft, loose material while in winter it is hard, dry pellets. While this change may be partly due to the low water content of the dry winter foods and to the restricted winter water intake of the animals, it also serves to conserve energy which the musk ox must use in winter to convert the snow it eats into water, and any conservation of energy in winter helps it to resist extreme cold.

The reproductive cycle of the musk ox is well adapted to the climatic extremes of its far north land. The breeding season begins in late June or early July and by the end of July the fighting between the bulls for a stable of cows is in full swing. The height of the rut occurs between the first and the third weeks in August, at a time when food is plentiful, the weather is reasonable, and the musk ox can put its energy to matters other than the gathering of food. Although there is no firm evidence to in-

dicate the actual period of gestation in wild musk ox it is believed to be eight to nine months long, with the calves being born over an extended period from the latter part of April to the first week in June, most calves appearing in May. At first glance this would seem to be a most inopportune time for a newborn calf to arrive on the tundra; at that time of year temperatures may be as low as minus 20 degrees Fahrenheit, especially on the far north ranges. But the musk ox calf is born with a thick coat of fur and, once dry, is well able to stand quite cold temperatures. What would be vastly more difficult would be to be born a few weeks later, when temperatures were higher, but when its chances of being exposed to freezing rain and wet snow along with high winds, would be quite high. Any such combination would mean certain death for even the hardy, newborn musk ox calf. Thus its early arrival is actually an adaptive feature to the realities of this cold land.

By being born at the very beginning of the summer period, the musk ox is able to take maximum advantage of the complete cycle of summer growth of the plants. Arctic plants spring to life very quickly in the early summer, often before the snow has left the ground; as the musk ox calf is able to browse on vegetation within a week after birth, it is able to start immediately to feed its growing body and to store up the energy it will need for the long winter ahead. The calf will suckle from the mother within a few minutes of birth and continue to take part of its food this way until it is as much as a year and a half old. This period of prolonged lactation provides the calf with extra food during its first long winter, when it might have difficulty obtaining enough to meet its needs for energy and growth.

Although the musk ox is a big animal it has very short appendages; its tail is only about four inches long and its legs are quite short and stocky, allowing quick circulation of blood from the body to these extremities and back, thus reducing heat loss in the limbs. Heat is further imprisoned within the musk ox by its almost complete covering of fur, the dense, fine inner hair and the much longer outer guard hairs. The combination of both provides excellent insulation and the guard hair, which is often so long it trails on the ground hiding the feet, provides shelter for the calf. The only bare skin the musk ox exposes to the elements is at the tip of its nose. In summer the fine, inner hair is shed (it is an excellent wool) allowing the animal to better cope with the higher temperatures.

The musk ox is a slow-moving animal, rarely given to flight over the tundra. When alarmed it usually goes into a type of stockade defence, either a circle like the famous circle of carts on the western plains, or a straight line, with the young and females taking up positions slightly behind the male defenders. The circle formation is an excellent defence against groups of wolves; the straight line is better for a single wolf. As the musk ox moves about feeding, it proceeds slowly, with great dignity, and this slowness of movement, plus the lack of a flight characteristic for defence, helps it to conserve energy and heat; a behavioral adaptation to the cold climate of the tundra biome.

One of the more comical (to the observer) traits of the adult musk ox bull is the form of displacement activity it adopts whenever threatened by sensed, but somewhat remote danger. Most birds and animals adopt some form of what science calls displacement activity, whenever they are stimulated to attack or to flee and can do neither. Under such conditions a male human will kick his dog, or slam his fist on the table, perhaps even beat his wife instead of his boss. A gull will freeze immobile in an attack attitude; a blackbird will peck at a leaf instead of the other bird. Whenever the adult bull musk ox is confronted by such a situation, as when a human observer sits in full view on a nearby hilltop not threatening but not going away, the bull, or bulls, will first pace out in front of the group where they paw at the earth and wipe their foreheads on their forefeet, which is the usual signal for a quick charge. And charge they do but, instead of charging the observer, the bull suddenly wheels and charges the nearest bull. Heads held low, the two seven-hundred pound bulls come together with a tremendous crash, which seems to bother neither of them for they back off, sometimes charge again, sometimes not, stand for a few moments and then resume feeding as though nothing had happened.

Adult musk oxen, because of the combination of adaptations they have made, seem able to withstand the coldest and most severe weather that can come their way. Curiously enough for such a well-adapted animal, the one winter condition that can cause them great hardship, and sometimes even death, is very deep snow, particularly if the snow has been interspersed with periods of freezing rain. Musk ox have a great deal of difficulty digging down through deep snow and a hard snow crust to get at their food. Although no records exist of such conditions causing excessive loss of life on the Arctic coast of Canada, it happened in Greenland during the winter of 1953-54 when hundreds, possibly thousands, of musk ox perished, unable to dig down through deep snow and an ice crust to get at their food.

Although most of the large Arctic mammals have the ability and the opportunity to move south during the winter, only certain of the mainland herds of caribou turn to migration as a means of escaping the bitter cold of the tundra biome; these herds move south into the sub-Arctic bush late in the autumn and do not return until the warmer weather of the following spring. Other herds remain on the open tundra, as do the groups of musk ox which tend to remain close to a home valley or set of hills all their lives. The polar bear roams freely over the ice of the Arctic seas but so firmly is it wedded to its Arctic environment that, although it may be carried far to the south in Hudson and James Bay on the drifting ice in the summer and often swims ashore to a beach beyond which lies the shelter of the sub-Arctic bush, it heads north again, not south, back to the ice and cold and food of its Arctic coast homeland. This is why there are no polar bears in the Antarctic, an area in which a polar bear could live a life of plenty; the polar bear developed in the north polar zone and is now unable to migrate the long distance south through the iceless and, to it, foodless, temperate and tropic zones between.

ANIMALS OF THE NORTHERN RANGE

Life is not easy in this ice-cold region, and a combination of morphological, physiological and behavioural adaptations have been made by animals to ensure survival. Sea mammals develop a thick layer of fat beneath the skin, as an insulation against the colder winter temperatures, as well as a source of energy when the food supply lessens. A few land animals enter a state of dormancy or complete hibernation, and there is a seasonal change in the density of the insulated body-coverings of some animals. Musk oxen (above) have roamed the interior in a nearly-perfect cold-adapted state for centuries.

The weasel lives in tunnels in the broken rock or shale.

The tundra wolf, master predator of the Arctic coast region, follows the caribou herds in their ceaseless movement over the land in search of food.

The Arctic ground squirrel, "Shik-Shik," tunnels in the ground.

The polar bear, king of the Arctic coast mammals, spends most of its life on or in the sea and, in summer, often swims in the open sea, many miles from the nearest land.

The harp seal, named for the harp design on its coat, inhabits only Hudson Strait and Frobisher Bay.

108

The huge Arctic hare changes from winter white to summer brown except in the northern islands where it remains white.

Caribou roam endlessly over the land, sometimes in small herds and sometimes in hundreds and thousands, as shown on the next page.

Arctic coast mammals of land and sea

Prior to the massive flow of glacial ice over northern North America mammals had intermingled freely across the top of the continent. However the advancing ice drove small groups of each species into refugia, each separated from the other by the ice. Each group, in its isolation, developed along slightly different lines; caribou were divided into a woodland species, a mountain species, a tundra species and a far northern species. Shrews of the Mackenzie and Yukon District developed differently from their relatives in the southeast. Walrus were divided into two species—the Atlantic and the Pacific— and they have remained divided to this day, although it is possible for walrus to pass across the top of North America into each other's range.

In summer, walrus "heave-out" onto certain rocky islands all through the Arctic. On land they are very vulnerable and easy prey for hunting man.

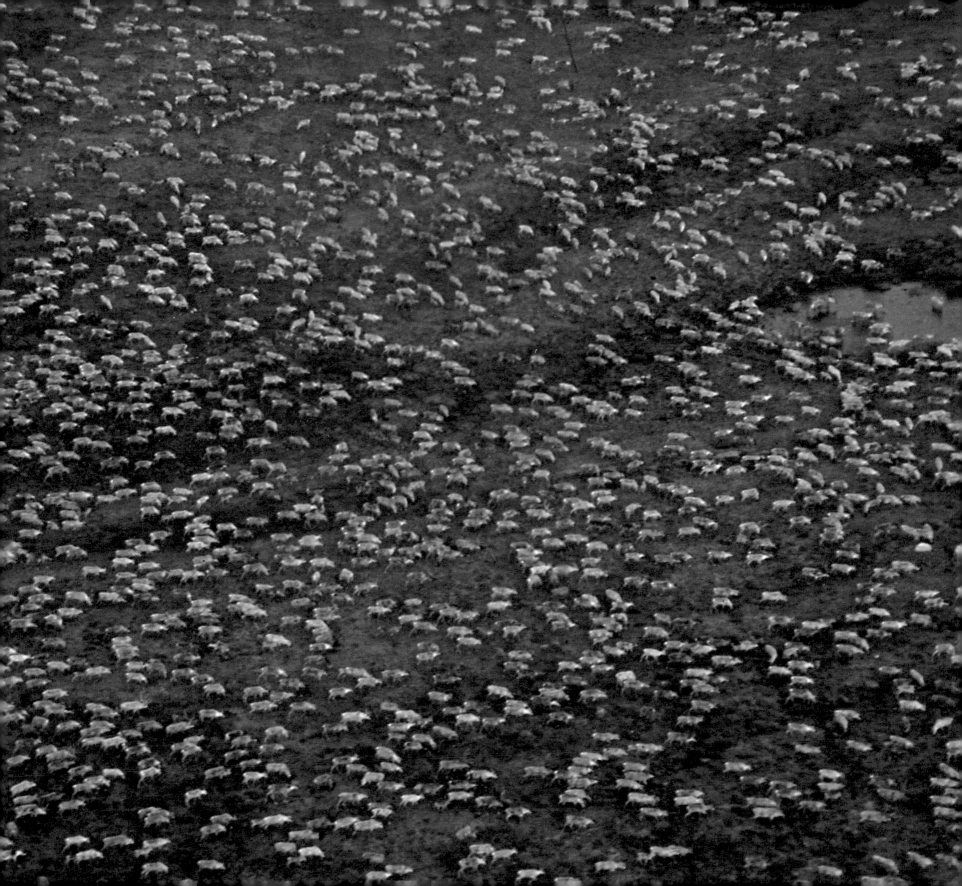

11 INVISIBLE WORLD OF THE ARCTIC COAST

Four hundred million years ago, during the time when much of North America was under water and thick accumulations of sediments were building up around the core of the great Canadian Shield, when plants were slowly spreading out over the virgin face of the exposed land and life in the seas was dominated by the primitive fishes, there lived in the coastal waters off the Arctic coast region of Canada species of the first of the true vertebrates to leave behind a fossil record of their existence —the Ostracoderms, aquatic, fish-like creatures up to several feet long. Ostracoderms were bottom dwellers, without jaws of any kind, most likely scooping or sucking up their food through a round opening in their heads. Their bodies were covered with bony scales, and, when they died, the scales resisted the efforts of the chemicals in the water to disintegrate them; they remained to be buried in the bottom sediments where they survive today, fossil evidence of the dominant form of life on the Arctic coast of 400 million years ago.

In the unimaginably long span of time that has passed since the Ostracoderms fed and bred in the waters off the Arctic coast, the outline and contour of North America has changed and re-changed many times; the climate, warm for so long, has gone from warm to cold, back to warm, back to cold, countless times. Flora of land and sea have come and gone, including the Ostracoderms. But one thing has not changed from those days of so long ago—on the Arctic coast creatures of the sea remain the dominant form of life.

Draw a map of your homeland and, almost without exception, you will trace an outline of the peninsulas and capes of the land; land upon which you were born, upon which you now live and travel; land from which you draw your sustenance and in which you will be buried when you die. But ask an Arctic coast Eskimo hunter to draw a map of his homeland and he will trace an outline of the bays and inlets of the sea; the sea which gives him the meat he needs for his food, the skins he needs for his boots and his clothing, the fat he uses for his heat and light; the sea, on the surface of which he will spend the greater part of his life. On paper his map will look the same as yours; in fact they represent two entirely different worlds.

A newcomer to the Arctic coast in winter could be pardoned for feeling that the attachment of the Eskimo hunter for his sea was badly misplaced; mile after mile the snow-covered ice stretches out to the distant horizon, a desert of white on which there is rarely any movement to indicate the presence of mammalian or other aquatic life. But this surface appearance is deceiving; invisible beneath the miles of land-fast ice along the Arctic coast swim hundreds of seals; almost as invisible out among the broken ice and open water of the central pack live some of the largest mammals in the world—the Greenland right whale, the white whale and the narwhal, along with the huge walrus and the mighty polar bear. Back of the coasts, beneath the six and eight foot thick ice of the larger Arctic lakes live the cold water adapted fishes, relatives of species to the south —schools of succulent Arctic char feed throughout the long winter; lake trout and whitefish prowl the waters beneath the ice for their food; graylings, even a few northern pike, swim in the rivers of the western Arctic that flow north to the Arctic sea.

Life is not easy in the cold waters beneath the non-land of the Arctic coast region, particularly in the waters of the Arctic seas. Fish are not found in great numbers anywhere off Arctic coasts; the great fisheries of the northern hemisphere occur in sub-Arctic waters, at the places where the cold Arctic currents meet and mingle with the warmer flows from the Atlantic and Pacific Oceans. In far north water the Arctic cod inhabits Hudson Bay and the seas off the lower Arctic islands; tom cod feed in the coastal waters off the northwest mainland coast as far east as Coronation Gulf; jackfish are abundant in the Mackenzie Delta. Arctic halibut seem to be moving into the waters of the Hudson Strait region; Atlantic cod increased off the west coast of Greenland all through the 1930's but began to decline in size and numbers late in the 1950's. This movement north and south of the Atlantic cod is an excellent indicator of changing water temperatures in the Arctic seas off the northeast coast of Canada. Atlantic cod feed in the shallows of the continental shelf, preferring water between two and four degrees Centigrade. Warming of the coastal water off the Arctic coast brings them north; cooling sends them south again.

The Arctic sea is home to several members of the sculpin family, and that ugly little fish, the stickleback. The only large fish of the Arctic coast is the Greenland shark, which has been appearing in ever-increasing numbers in the waters of the north-eastern Arctic all through the past decade. They seem to be especially abundant off north Baffin Island and in the Lancaster-Jones Sound region. This shark loves the cold waters of the far north; it grows to be some ten to twelve feet long but has a very small brain and is quite sluggish in the water. Its meat is toxic to humans when fresh; its main asset seems to be its huge liver, up to seven feet long in an adult fish, from which can be extracted an oil rich in Vitamin A.

In the tidal zone of the Arctic, sea life has difficulty maintaining itself; every spring, when the sea ice breaks up, huge chunks grind back and forth over the rocks and across the sandy bottom. No sessile animal is safe from being crushed off the rocks by this ice movement. A few limpets may exist in the deep clefts, along with a few amphipods and a stray fish species or two, but there are few hiding places for them in the tidal zone although worms, copepods and ostrapods are found in shallow bays that are protected from ice scour by sandbars across the entrances.

It is the lakes of the Arctic that harbour the greatest variety and numbers of fish. Whitefish and huge lake trout occur in all the larger lakes; Arctic grayling inhabit the swift flowing streams of the western Arctic; northern pike have been taken from the estuary of the Coppermine River and in certain lakes on Boothia Peninsula. An unusual fish is found in a lake a short distance inland from the south shore of Frobisher Bay—a school of Arctic cod, fish of the sea, that have become trapped in the lake. The lake has a layer of fresh water on top of a layer of salt water in which the cod live, feeding on themselves. In the past the very high tides in Frobisher Bay brought sea-water flooding into the lake and presumably brought in the cod as well. With the continued, slow rise of the land in this area, the flooding occurred less and less often; the fish have now become trapped in the lake.

The dominant fish of the Arctic coast region is the Arctic char, a member of the salmon family, not unlike the Atlantic salmon in appearance. Red fleshed, with lots of fat on the body, the average size adult char weighs from four to six pounds, although it can grow to eighteen pounds. The char spends most of its life in the fresh water of the inland lakes; in certain lakes along the west coast of Hudson Bay, where access to the sea has been cut off by the rising of the land, the char is a completely freshwater fish. But most char go down to the sea for a few weeks in summer soon after the fifth year of their life. On these moves from the lakes to the sea and return, they move in large schools, down the rivers in June, back up the same rivers about mid-August. Not all lake and river systems have runs of Arctic char but those that do are well known to the Eskimo hunters of the area.

In the cold waters of the Arctic coast region it is the sea mammals that have evolved as the dominant life forms. Seals, walrus, whales are all mammals—warm-blooded, air breathing animals which suckle their young. All have developed special methods of breathing while living their entire lives in the Arctic seas. All have limbs that are adapted to serve as paddles and rudders to propel them through the water; some are able to use them in a limited way to provide locomotion on land or on ice. The adaptations to cold they have made are somewhat different from those made by their fellow mammals on land. Land mammals have had to exist in a region where temperatures ranged from sixty degrees above to sixty below, where vicious winds robbed their bodies of vital heat and energy. The mammals of the sea had no such problems to face. The temperature of the Arctic sea-water is cold, but not very cold, all year round with only slight variations in seasonal norms. Thus the sea mammals were able to adapt to a much simpler set of Arctic conditions within their watery environment.

Nevertheless, the adaptations they made were surprisingly similar to those of the land mammals. They have no fur; some have no hair at all on their bodies, others have short, bristly hair. But all do have great layers of fat beneath the skin to serve as insulation in place of fur, and also to serve as a source of energy if food supplies get low. This layer of fat thickens and thins with the season, very thick by the end of the winter, thinner during the late summer, so thin in the ringed seals that they lose much of their usual buoyancy in the water and sink quickly when killed; during autumn and spring they float like corks. The sea

The Arctic char, favourite food of Eskimo hunters, has migrated up and down the same well-known Arctic coast rivers for generations.

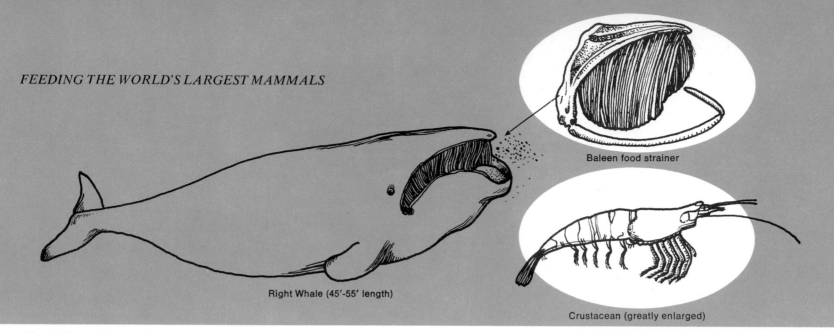

Baleen food strainer

Right Whale (45'-55' length)

Crustacean (greatly enlarged)

The right, or baleen whale strains its food from the sea water by using a unique sieve-like structure of baleen, found within its jaws.

mammals are squat and torpedo-shaped, with short extremities; like the land mammals, the temperature within the extremities is different from that of the rest of the body.

One special adaptation of the ringed seal is a birth cycle phenomenon known as delayed implantation, which plays an important role in the life cycle of this seal. Ringed seals are born live, with the mother in a cave under the snow on top of the ice. Usually only one pup is born at a time and the mother suckles it for several months after birth, first in the cave and later in the water. The seal's milk is very rich in fat, containing up to ten times as much as cow's milk; on such a rich diet the young seal grows very quickly. Within a very short time after birth of her young the female mates again, but the growth of the new embryo does not begin immediately; the embryo remains in a rudimentary condition for several weeks with very little sign of any growth occurring in the uterus during this time. The length of the delay in the beginning of development is timed so that the entire birth cycle takes almost exactly one year, with the baby being born in the spring to the mother in her snow cave on the sea ice and ready for almost instant mating again. The larger bearded seal and the walrus have a birth cycle that takes a little over one year to complete; the female cannot mate until the year following birth and young bearded seals and walrus are born only in alternate years to the same mother.

The largest of the Arctic coast sea mammals are the huge whales, but these are no longer plentiful in the north polar region. The last great herds were hunted almost to extinction in the Beaufort Sea, Baffin Bay and Hudson Bay late in the nineteenth and early in the twentieth centuries. Occasional sightings are reported by Eskimos on north Baffin Island but, after almost two centuries of relentless pursuit and killing in all the seas of the northern hemisphere, the large whales may be so reduced in numbers that they are gone forever, too few in numbers to do anything but eventually vanish completely from our northern coasts.

These large whales were all toothless, generally called baleen whales, because of the special, sieve-like structures within their mouths that allowed them to gulp in great quantities of sea-water as they swam along, straining from the water the small invertebrates they ate for food. The smaller whales left in the Arctic are all toothed; they have rows of teeth in their jaws that allow them to catch fish and other marine creatures. The largest is the most ferocious—the killer whale, an aptly-named monster that will attack almost anything moving in the water. Black above and white below, with a large black fin that cuts through the water in front of a white wake when the whale is moving at speed near the surface, the killer whale of the Arctic coast eats seals and other small whales. But it can kill the larger whales by

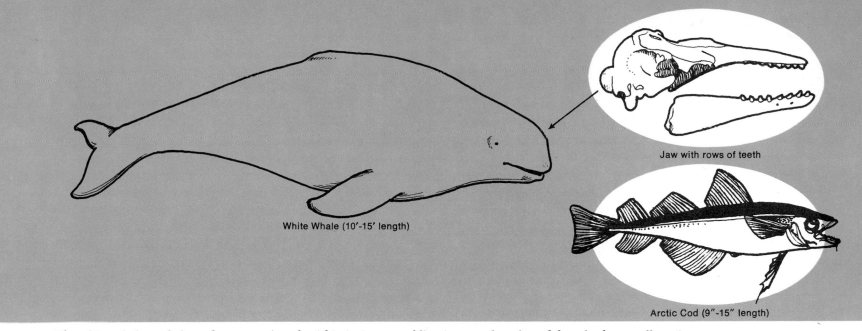

White Whale (10'-15' length)

Jaw with rows of teeth

Arctic Cod (9"-15" length)

The white whale, or beluga, has rows of teeth within its jaws, enabling it to catch and eat fish and other small marine creatures.

forcing open their mouths and tearing out the tongues. It will also stalk man if he is in a kayak on the water, or if he is walking on the sea ice near open water in which the whale can surface. Killer whales have been known to stalk beneath the thinner ice near the floe edge and then come up under the ice to try to break it and dump the man into the water.

The most common whale of the Arctic coast is the white whale, or Beluga, milk-white in colour, usually about ten to fifteen feet long. The white whale has no back fin; it propels itself through the water by means of a large, horizontal fluked tail and steers by means of short fins on either side of its body near the head. Breathing is accomplished through a blow hole on the top of the head while the whale is lying on the surface or cruising along in a series of shallow dives. White whales, like all Cetaceans, are highly intelligent and lead complex social lives. Sight is not well developed in these mammals but hearing is; their ears are basically similar to ours but far keener and they use a system of radar, like the bats, to locate undersea objects. White whales communicate constantly—British tars called them "sea canaries"—sound issuing through the puckered-up breathing hole in the top of the head from a sound chamber within the great bulge of the forehead.

White whales leave the Arctic coast waters in the winter and are seen off the east coast of North America as far south as Cape

Cod. As soon as the bays and inlets are free of ice on the north coast they return to spend the summer feeding along the coasts and in the estuaries of large rivers, occasionally penetrating the larger lakes that have a direct connection with the sea. Every so often white whales will be trapped in such a lake, or at the bottom end of a long fiord, by new ice forming early in the fall across the mouth of the inlet or across the outlet of the lake. As they must come up to breathe at an absolute maximum of every twenty minutes, and as they seem unwilling to navigate long distances under solid ice, they cannot escape. Inexorably the ice closes in over the open water of the lake or the fiord, up into which they must rise to breathe. Unless found and killed by hunters the trapped whales will all die, as did a group of whales caught in the Eskimo Lakes of the Mackenzie Delta district in the winter of 1966-67.

The strangest of the Arctic whales is the narwhal—the unicorn of the Arctic seas. Narwhal have been known to western man for centuries but science is still not sure about the tusk of the narwhal. Although both sexes have two rudimentary tusks, only in the male does the left one develop beyond the jaw to protrude as a long, spirally grooved, and often twisted, tusk of ivory that can be up to ten feet long. About one male in fifty or sixty will develop the right tusk in addition to the left but it will only be about a third of the length of the left. The tusk is an overgrown canine tooth and is hollow with the dental canal reaching almost to the tip. The ivory is quite brittle and it is common to find narwhal with a portion of the end of the tusk broken off. Eskimos of north Baffin Island claim that narwhal have toothache in the tusk and often break them off near the tip while scraping them on the rocks to relieve the pain. They also claim that the narwhal uses the tusk to stir up tom cod, sculpin and other food from the sea bottom and to spear big fish when feeding far from shore. Certainly the tusk must be used in some way for it is always well polished near the tip. Some scientists believe that it serves no practical purpose at all, that it is a secondary sexual ornament adorning the male.

I've hunted and photographed narwhals from my kayak many times on the waters of Eclipse Sound but my most thrilling involvement with a narwhal occurred while I was sitting on a rocky hilltop on the east coast of the sound scanning the broken ice surface in late June watching and listening for the first narwhal movement into the bays. As my telescope panned slowly across what seemed to be an unbroken stretch of flat ice, but which I knew would be laced with cracks of open water I could not see from afar, I was startled to see rising up through the ice the thrashing form of a huge narwhal. Higher and higher it rose in the air until the big head, with its ten foot long tusk, shook and danced in weird rhythm a dozen feet above the ice surface. Suddenly the whale slid rapidly back down into the water and was gone, and I knew that a killer whale hunted below the ice, driving the narwhal into such a state of terror that it had tried to climb out of the water onto the surface of the ice above.

The killer whale also preys on the huge walrus, but it prefers to eat the young animals rather than the old. With its twin tusks of ivory a large walrus is a formidable foe; there is nothing else that will tackle an adult male walrus in the water except the killer whale, although the polar bear will attack walrus on land where they are more vulnerable. Eskimos tell stories of walrus attacks on hunters in kayaks; they will attack canoes and whaleboats, even forty foot Peterhead boats. The walrus attempts to hook its tusks over the gunwale of the boat and tip the occupants into the water. An enraged walrus will attack with tusks, and by bunting with its big head, charges in repeatedly with all the skill and agility of a sea "goat."

Large walrus can be ten to twelve feet in length and weigh up to two and a half tons. The outer hide of the adult is so tough that it quickly blunts the edge of the big knife used to cut up an animal after killing. The walrus is a highly gregarious mammal; the sexes are usually segregated with the older males keeping together in herds and the adult females with young of both sexes forming a separate group. While sleeping on the ice pans, or hauled out on the rocky islands, walrus huddle together in tightly-packed "pods," although lone bulls are common. The walrus pup is born in the late spring; it swims immediately but it spends a good deal of the time during the first weeks riding about on its mother's back. When she dives deep to feed, the pup clings to the front flippers. The mother, indeed the entire herd, treats the young with a great deal of care and lavishes much affection on them. The pup nurses from the mother for up to two years as it must await the development of its tusks before it can begin to root around on the sea bottom for its food—clams and other mollusks. The life expectancy of a healthy walrus can be as much as twenty years.

An unusual feature of the walrus is that certain individuals, for reasons not yet clearly understood, deviate from their usual diet to become predators of the sea, feeding on the meat and fat of ringed seals, bearded seals, even small whales. The act of predation has never been witnessed by a biologist but tales of walrus killing seals abound in Eskimo folklore and contemporary stories, and remains of sea mammals have been found in the stomachs of dead walrus. Such walrus are almost always males, solitary bulls that are lean and slender in build with exceptionally well developed shoulders and forelimbs. Their tusks are long, slender and very sharp, often covered with scratches. Eskimos say that these walrus become carnivores when they are orphaned during the first year or two of their lives and, being without tusks, they turn to scavenging and preying on whatever they can kill. In effect, they adapt to a condition of "no-tusks," and continue as predators for the rest of their lives.

A number of different types of seals inhabit the coastal waters of the Arctic but only two can be considered as true Arctic species—the huge bearded seal and the much smaller ringed seal. Harp seals, the hunting of which caused such an uproar over killing methods alleged to be employed by the sealers, are not commonly seen in the Arctic coast region except in the Frobisher Bay—Hudson Strait area in summer. The hooded seal is seen even less; it is usually found in the heavy pack ice far out in Baffin Bay, Davis Strait and the north Atlantic. The hooded seal gets its name from a bag-like swelling on the end of the male seal's nose, which is inflated whenever it becomes angry. With bladder inflated the hooded seal is almost as fierce an antagonist as an enraged walrus.

The bearded seal, or square flipper, is a huge animal up to ten feet long, weighing as much as eight hundred pounds. Although as long as a walrus it is much slimmer and lacks the tusks. It is a seal of the open water and ice, but it will live under the land-fast ice in winter, keeping open its own breathing holes or using those of the smaller ringed seal. It is a solitary animal, usually seen swimming alone in the dark green waters or asleep,

on solitary ice pans. Only at breeding time does it gather into groups. The pups are born late in March, covered with dark grey, mottled hair.

If the dominant life form of the Arctic seas of four hundred million years ago was the Ostracoderm, today that honour must go to the ringed seal, the most widely distributed sea mammal of the north polar region, found in the sea all along the Arctic coasts wherever there is land-fast ice on which it can breed. The ringed seal, or jar as it is often called, is one link in a food chain of the sea.

In the sea the microscopic diatoms correspond to the vegetation of the land, converting sunlight that filters down through the upper layers of the water into energy through photosynthesis,

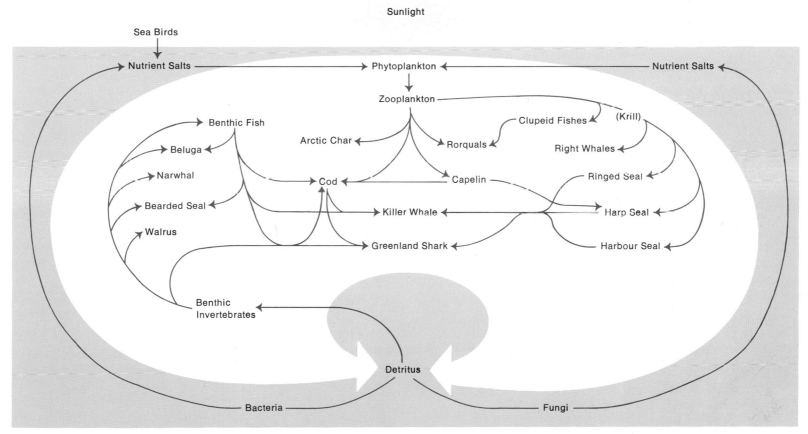

This simplified, biological cycle of life in northern seas shows (see white crescent-shaped area above) that directly or indirectly, all marine creatures, algae and the bottom-dwelling Benthic invertebrates eventually become organic detritus.

creating rich "pastures" in which certain sea life grazes. Although the Arctic seas receive no sunlight in winter the long day of summer makes up for this deficit, and everywhere the sea is not covered over by heavy ice, there is a great multiplying of the diatoms during the month of August; often the water is stained brown with their mass. Their growth is helped by the fact that cold water contains a high concentration of polymerized water molecules, which has a beneficial effect on the division and growth of plant cells.

Feeding directly on the diatoms are the plankton—larval stages of mollusks, worms and crustaceans, the copepods of the sea, and certain young fish. The cold water plankton of the Arctic seas is remarkable for the large size of the individual, compared with the same or related species inhabiting waters farther south; even in the sea there seems to be a general adherence to the rule that large size benefits all fauna in a cold region. The most common food of the ringed seal are two small, shrimp-like crustaceans; mysis, inhabiting the bottom layers of the deeper waters, and misto, a free-swimming crustacean. By utilizing both types, and supplementing its diet with small fish like polar cod, the ringed seal is able to live almost everywhere in Arctic coast waters.

In summer ringed seals swim about in the ice free waters, sometimes hauling out on shore if there are no convenient ice floes about. In winter many move out to the open sea beyond the edge of the land-fast ice where they swim and feed along the floe edge. But others remain in the sounds, bays and inlets that are completely covered over by six to seven foot thick ice. In order to breathe, each seal keeps open a series of holes in the thick ice. Starting in the autumn, when the new ice is forming on the surface of the sea, the seal rises up beneath the thin, pliable sea ice cover and pushes up a small mound of ice which cracks sufficiently for a small hole to form in the top. The seal lies vertical beneath the ice with its nose in the small air space between the ice and the water surface. It repeats this procedure at a number of places and, over the period of days while the new forming ice is thickening and losing its pliability, the seal visits each hole regularly, to breathe and to keep it from freezing over. All winter long it keeps up this constant movement from hole to hole while the ice about grows thicker and thicker. By spring each hole will be a vertical tunnel through the ice; on the surface the initial tiny hole, now buried beneath a hard packed drift, has been enlarged so that the seal is able to put its head above the water surface but still be invisible to anyone above.

Early in March the female seal enlarges one of the breathing holes with her teeth and the sharp claws of her front flippers, usually a hole that lies beneath a patch of broken ice over which the winter snow will have piled in deep drifts. The seal comes out onto the ice surface under the snow and hollows out a cave, in which the young seal is born, usually at any time through the period late March to mid-April. At birth the seal pup weighs about ten pounds and is covered with a thick coat of curly, white fur which it begins to shed after two weeks. A baby seal is not unlike a human infant with tiny, almost human face, and its large, shoe-button eyes; its cries are similar to those of a new-born human infant. By the time it is six weeks old it has shed its baby hair completely and is covered with finely textured hair, silvery on the belly, dark grey on the back on which the first traces of the adult pattern of circles can be seen—the "silver jar" of the trader.

As soon as the hot sun has begun to melt the snow cover, the seal enlarges the openings over its breathing holes so that it can pull itself out of the water onto the ice surface. Here it sleeps in the sun on warm, windless days, raising its head every few seconds to look about for danger. Although exceptionally alert for anything that could cause them harm, ringed seals are inquisitive creatures; they can be kept on the ice surface, while a dog team and sled rush madly at them over the ice, by a long sustained cry which seems to arouse their curiosity as to what on earth it could be coming at them over the ice. While swimming on the open sea they are easily lured in close by soft noises, a whistle, or a sharp knock on the side of a boat.

Ringed seals mature when they are seven years of age, although females sometimes become pregnant at five to six years old. Only rarely are they found among the floating pack ice of the open ocean; their range is the sheltered waters along the coasts. Their main predators are few but, unfortunately for the seal, they are all very proficient. The killer whale hunts the seal beneath the sea and, on the surface of water and ice alike, they are hunted by two of their most implacable enemies—the huge, white ghost of the Arctic coast, the mighty polar bear, and by that most proficient of all predators—hunting man.

INVASION FROM THE SOUTH

Nearly a thousand years ago, a small band of Viking voyagers left their settlement on the west coast of Greenland to sail across the expanse of Baffin Bay. European explorers followed the Norse; whalers followed explorers; traders and developers, like this snowmobiler on Frobisher Bay, all arrived in turn, each a disrupting influence on the basic ecological pattern of the land. Technological advances have made it possible to exist in relative comfort in a land dominated by cold.

Bulldozer "rolling" an airstrip on frozen lake during blizzard.

A portable heater warms the inside of the airplane in sub-zero weather.

The changing Arctic

Western man's bulldozers build roads, airfields, townsites, but they also rip up the tundra and disturb the permafrost, setting in motion forces that could destroy the delicately balanced Arctic communities of flora and fauna. Settlements dump pollutants into air and water and his competitive and acquisitive social system leaves little room for understanding the way of life of the Arctic hunter, and so his culture heads down the road to oblivion.

right: This young Eskimo girl cashier in a supermarket at Frobisher Bay, Southern Baffin Island, is better housed, better fed, better "educated" than her hunter forebears; what does her future hold on the Arctic coast of Canada?

Bulldozer tracks scar the ground at a Melville Island oil well.

A utilidor system for water and sewage lines in the town of Inuvik.

Winter fuel oil supply, part of man's life-line from the south, covers a beach on north Baffin Island.

PART FIVE/ CONSERVATION

12 A LAND OF FEAST OR FAMINE

The month was February, the year 1954, the place—north Baffin Island, out on the snow and ice-covered surface of Tay Sound to be exact. With my Eskimo "father," Idlouk, I was travelling by sled through the darkness of a midwinter "day" checking fox traps set on the headlands and tiny estuaries jutting from the high walls of rock that flank the upper reaches of the fiord. For nine months I had been living with Idlouk and his family at their camp near the bottom of Eclipse Sound, trying to find out what it was like to exist on the Arctic coast as an Eskimo hunter with only the natural resources of a high north land to provide clothing, transportation, shelter and food. On this particular trip I was learning a lot; it was four days since we had left camp and in that time the temperature had stayed steady at about 45° below zero. For three of the four days we had taken no foxes from the traps; for the past two days we had eaten nothing at all, having been unsuccessful in our attempts to shoot hares on the moonlit slopes or seals at their breathing holes in the thick ice of the sound. I was near numb with cold, and hungry enough to eat my caribou skin boots, bearskin bottoms and all.

Late that night as I lay sleepless, cold and hungry in my caribou skin sleeping robe inside our tiny overnight snowhouse, it dawned on me that I was an active participant in one of the famous, or infamous, feast and famine cycles which are a characteristic phenomenon in the natural life of the fauna of the Arctic coast. The significance of what was happening began to filter through a fog of misunderstanding built up over thirty-odd years of growing up as an urbanite, part of a technological society which had gained a large measure of control over its natural environment; enough control that, as an individual within that society, I felt I could ignore the complex relationships that exist between all living elements of the natural world. In southern Canada my relationships with the flora and fauna were casual and often long range; neither seemed important to my continued existence. But, living the life of an Eskimo hunter on north Baffin Island, I was brought face to face with a basic reality—as a human mammal I was only one element in a struc-

ture of elements, bound by invisible threads into an interdependent relationship with the natural world around me. On this trip I couldn't connect one of the threads; I couldn't shoot a rabbit or a seal that I needed for my food and because of this I was cold and hungry; if I didn't get meat soon I would die.

That night on north Baffin Island my relationship with the natural world around me underwent a subtle change. Physically and emotionally, as well as intellectually, I joined the world of the mammals on earth, no longer simply a human, but a human mammal, subject to certain basic laws of supply and demand that govern all life in the mammalian world. For the first time it was being brought home to me very forcefully that, as an individual separate from the natural world around me, I could not exist; I lived only because of the transmission of energy through the invisible, pyramidal systems that scientists call food chains. And with this realization came new understanding; no longer did I feel myself set over against my Arctic environment. With Idlouk and the other Eskimo hunters of the area, I became as one with the seals and the walrus and the caribou, and the life forms of land and sea on which they fed; I became as one with the huge mass of the invisible sun, source of all life and energy on the planet earth.

The next day we still couldn't get food but, late in the afternoon, our sled rounded a rock point of land beyond which we could see a tiny pinpoint of yellow light. Immediately the dogs howled and broke into a run pulling the sled, bumping and crashing, through the rough ice of the tidal zone onto a gently sloping beach. From a mound of snow that almost completely concealed their sod and sealskin house, Eskimo neighbours poured forth to help us unload the sled and release the dogs. Within a matter of minutes Idlouk and I were squatting inside the low, dimly lit house thawing our near frozen faces and feet, wolfing down raw caribou and seal meat from a food box in the corner. Three cups of hot tea later I lay on the caribou-skin-covered sleeping platform jammed in among eight other tired souls. Body recharged with vital energy, I drifted off to happy sleep.

Our natural world thrives on energy; energy that originates in the sun and flows out to pervade all living matter. But different forms of life can use the energy from the sun only when it is available to them in a form they can assimilate within their

Our natural world thrives on energy, which originates in the sun and flows out to pervade all living matter.

structures. I can't exist on raw energy from the sun but plants can, and certain plants can convert this energy into a form that my body can assimilate and use. So I eat these plants, or I eat the meat of other mammals that eat the plants, and I am really eating energy from the sun; I am part of a simple food chain. The term, chain, is a little misleading, for a chain is usually a set of orderly links fastened securely one to the other. In nature a "chain" is often a very complex structure in which links are fastened to other links in a bewildering array of patterns and designs. Particularly is this true in the temperate and tropic zones of earth, where the diversity of life forms seems almost endless. On the Arctic coast life forms are few in number and often simple in form; thus they have a clear "chain" structure that ties them inextricably one to the other and binds them all to their Arctic home environment.

In the Arctic coast region, as over all the world, the beginning link in the food chain is the sun. Although the Arctic is without the sun for a part of the year in most localities, it recoups much of this loss by having sunlight for extra long periods during the summer months, when for twenty-four hours a day light pours onto the Arctic vegetation—the lowly lichens, the mosses, the grasses, the plants, the bushes—which gathers in the energy and transforms it into green growth through a process known as photosynthesis. Much of the energy is used up by the plants themselves in their own processes of growth and development; the plants are the primary consumers. But they also condense a portion of the energy and store it within their cells and this stored energy becomes available to a host of secondary consumers—certain insects, birds and mammals. The insects extract the energy from the nectar; the birds obtain it from the seeds and shoots; the herbivorous mammals eat the leaves, stalks and roots of the plants. Meagre as it may be by southern standards, Arctic vegetation brings life to the tundra community.

The herbivorous animals are the big secondary consumers of the energy; caribou eat mosses and lichens during the winter months, willows, birch, grass and sedges in addition to the moss and lichen in the summer. Musk ox eat almost anything that grows on the tundra although their food preferences will vary with the season. The Arctic hare feeds on a wide variety of plants – saxifrage, crowberry, grass and sedges; the ground squirrel eats mostly leaves, roots and seeds of the plants, as do the lemmings; meadow mice prefer green vegetation with roots and bark. The secondary consumers also use up much of the energy they get from the plants in their own processes of growth and development, but they, too, store an excess in the tissues of their bodies where it becomes available to a third level of consumer – the predator, insect, bird or mammal which has developed the specialization of obtaining its energy from the stored energy in the fat and flesh of its fellow insects, birds and animals.

The huge wolf of the tundra lives mainly on caribou, although it will turn to eating ground squirrels, mice and birds' eggs if it cannot get enough caribou meat to fill its belly. The fox feeds on eggs, young birds, mice and lemmings, often digging down through the winter snow with great speed to get the lemmings it hears running about in their tunnels underneath. The weasel darts among the rocks and shale of the tundra hills eating mice and lemmings it is able to trap and catch in the burrows. The shrew is the insectivore of the Arctic coast, its numerous, sharp-pointed teeth enable it to crush the hard-bodied beetles, the spiders and centipedes and, on occasion, a mouse or a lemming that has been caught in a trap. The snowy owl eats mice and lemmings; the gyrfalcon hunts ptarmigan on the slopes; jaegers eat eggs and young birds; the tern takes small fish from the lakes and the sea. As for the raven, it just isn't very fussy; it will eat almost anything at all.

The insects have special relationships with the mammals, both large and small. Mosquitoes draw the blood they must have in order to reproduce, from the caribou, musk ox, wolves and foxes, attacking these animals on the lips, ears, around the eyes and muzzle, on any bare patches of skin rubbed free of fur during the annual moult. Mites and lice use lemmings and mice

as living hosts; fleas breed in the thick, soft coats of the Arctic hare. Worms, spiders, midges, flies find food in the droppings of the smaller mammals and find breeding places in their burrows and nests. The blowfly utilizes the carcasses of lemmings and mice as a principle breeding ground, wherever no carcasses of the larger mammals can be found. In one recorded instance well over two hundred blowflies emerged from the tiny carcass of one dead lemming.

Warble flies begin life as eggs deposited on the legs or rump of the caribou by the parent in the months of July and August. The eggs develop into larvae which immediately burrow in under the skin of the animal and make their way along the back. Over the winter they live in the fat beneath the skin, growing in size until about as big as a bumble bee. The following June they burrow out through the hide to drop on the ground of the caribou range where they pupate to emerge a few weeks later as warble flies, that immediately lay more eggs on more caribou. Warble flies are the scourge of the caribou of the tundra; one animal can have as many as 350 larvae living within its flesh.

Operating in a wider cycle of parasitic life is the tiny tapeworm, *echinococcus granulosis,* which begins life as one of millions of tiny eggs deposited in the intestines of dogs, foxes or wolves by the adult tapeworm. The eggs are dropped onto the feeding range of the caribou in the faeces of the host, where they may lie for many months, later to be picked up and ingested by caribou browsing over the range. In the caribou the eggs hatch into larvae which migrate to the liver and other parts of the body where they form into cysts; in the brain or lungs such cysts bring death to the host animal.

Along the food chains of the tundra biome energy flows from the plants to the insects, to the birds, to the mammals. So long as all links of the chain remain intact the flow continues; life is born, it multiplies, it dies, in an endless cycle that has almost no beginning and almost no end. From sun to plant to insect, bird and mammal, the energy flows in seemingly inexhaustible supply; numbers of individuals multiply, more than enough to replace those dying of old age or accident, disease or predation. Certain species multiply slowly towards an optimum number that is seldom reached over the immense range of their tundra home. But others multiply and multiply, until suddenly there comes a year when there are too many individuals on the range and, over specific areas of the tundra biome, there occur great dyings-off of these species and their predators. One year the land teems with hares or lemmings; the next there will be almost none. Foxes are abundant for a year or two and then there will be almost none for a while. These regular cycles of plenty and scarcity are an ever-recurring phenomenon of the Arctic coast region; for most Arctic mammals the tundra biome is a vast land under constant alternation between plenty and want, a land of feast or famine.

The cycle of scarcity–plenty has been accurately plotted over many years for certain species of mammals and birds. The best documented is that of the fox, for fox skins are a staple item of trade at all Arctic posts and careful records are kept of the numbers of pelts handled each year. Everywhere on the Arctic coast there is a regular cycle in the numbers of foxes; they build to a peak population every four years, followed immediately by a rapid decline. The phases of the cycle do not match all across the Arctic; scarcity in one sector coincides with plenty in others; but the cycle occurs regularly everywhere, year after year after year, the direct result of a break in the links of a basic food chain.

Lemmings eat tundra vegetation; foxes and snowy owls eat lemmings—a simple food chain. Lemmings have one or more litters, of from four to six kits each, during the year, consequently they multiply rather quickly. But the tundra is wide and there is a lot of food in it for lemmings. In addition, the increase in their food supply stimulates the sex glands of the lemming predators, the snowy owl and the fox, in ways that are not yet clearly understood. In the owl it seems that the simple fact of excess visual sightings of lemmings stimulates areas of the brain that control secretions of the pituitary gland that controls the degree of sexual activity and the number of eggs produced by the female bird—the more lemmings seen by the snowy owls means the higher the production of snowy owls which will eat more lemmings. Similarly, in times of lemming abundance the foxes increase the numbers born in each litter, and there is usually a migration movement of foxes from other areas into the region of plenty, all helping to swell the numbers of the predators.

But it is the lemmings which increase the fastest. Despite the

Lemmings live on sun-nourished vegetation and, in turn, themselves become food for the Arctic fox and the snowy owl, to complete a simple food chain.

A shortage of lemmings, a basic food of the snowy owl, can drive the beautiful birds far south of their normal range.

ever-intensifying predation lemmings increase much faster than they die or are killed off. Three years after the time when lemmings were scarce on the land, the region teems with them. Because they live on a restricted range all their lives the pressure on the food supply in the area becomes prohibitive, as does the pressure of overcrowding on the lemmings themselves. Lemmings scurry everywhere across the tundra, preyed upon by owls, jaegers, foxes, wolves, dogs, even bears. Frantically they begin to leave their home range; almost blindly they swarm over the tundra, swimming across lakes and swift flowing rivers to leave hundreds drowned along the banks. In some sectors of the tundra biome, principally in Scandinavia and Alaska where the number of litters born to a single female in one year can be as high as eight, at the peak of the cycle millions of lemmings stream en masse across the tundra, swimming lakes and rivers, sometimes swimming to their deaths in ritual parade out into the open sea. Starved for food, frustrated into a state of nervous exhaustion through overcrowding, they die in their thousands. Next year the tundra is almost empty of lemmings, and of the foxes and owls which depend on them as food. Many foxes have died, others have migrated to different sectors of the tundra where lemmings are not yet in short supply. The snowy owls abandon their tundra range in the winter to appear far south in the woods and fields of southern Canada, searching for the food they cannot find in their far north home.

Shortage of food undoubtedly plays a major role in the dying-off of the lemmings. But overcrowding plays an equally important role. It is well known that simple overcrowding among humans and rodents causes stress to develop within the individual of the species with its typical effect on the nervous system, on the sex and the adrenal glands. When overcrowded, lemmings develop swollen adrenal glands and shrunken sex glands. The shrunken sex glands means that the male produces less sperm, the female produces fewer eggs; the mating urge decreases and fewer young will be conceived; of those conceived, more will die in the uterus, fewer will survive the first days after being born due to a shortage of milk from the mother. Because the hormones secreted by the adrenal cortex reduce inflammation and because inflammation is a defence mechanism of the body against infection, a lemming with an overactive adrenal gland is much more liable to invasion by bacteria and viruses, thus increasing greatly the possibility of its succumbing to infectious diseases. The effect of stimulation of the adrenal cortex is cumulative; if the stress developed through overcrowding is continued indefinitely, the adrenal gland becomes exhausted and the ability of the lemming to resist any adverse situation is drastically reduced; excess heat, excess cold, simple food shortage will very quickly cause death. And death comes quickly to the thousands and thousands of lemmings.

They die because they have eaten up most of the food on their range; they die by predation under attacks of the birds and mammals; they drown in their hundreds. They die of disease, excess heat, excess cold. And because they die their predators die, or they migrate away, and the land over which they fled and fought becomes empty almost overnight. A few lemmings remain, just enough to begin the cycle all over again.

Only one other mammal invades the tundra biome in numbers to match the lemming—the barren ground caribou. The caribou of the Arctic is a link in another simple food chain; caribou eat the mosses, lichens and grasses; wolves (and hunting man) eat the caribou. Unlike the lemming which lives on a restricted home range until driven from it by the pressures of overpopulation, the caribou roams the Arctic tundra constantly, for it is a big animal and they are many; their food supply does not grow tall and it grows again but slowly. To stay alive the caribou must spend its life on the move. Two species live on the Arctic coast—the barren ground caribou of the mainland and lower Arctic islands and the Peary caribou of the high Arctic islands, smaller than its southern cousin, white in general colour rather than brown with splashes of white.

Although most of the barren ground caribou migrate in great herds south into the trees for the winter, other mainland groups, and all those of the Arctic islands, remain on the tundra all winter, protected from the cold by their winter pelage of dense, erect hollow-stemmed hair which covers almost every part of the animal. The extremities of the caribou are short and the body stocky which gives it a short circulation course with minimum cooling of the blood and minimum body surface exposed to the biting winds. The cloven hoofs are round in outline, unlike those of southern deer which are always pointed; the hoofs splay out to form a wide snowshoe somewhat larger than a man's hand with fingers extended, which provides excellent support on the snow. Sharp edges on the hoofs give the caribou good traction on every type of surface except glare ice and provide it with efficient digging tools for scraping down through the hard packed winter snow cover to get at the moss and lichen on which it feeds. In the caribou, unlike southern deer, both sexes have antlers which differ from those of deer to the south by having a brow tine—a long, shovel-like projection that extends down over the forehead between the eyes.

On the mainland tundra the first thaw of spring usually comes late in April or early in May. By that time the herds of barren ground caribou, that have spent the winter in the forests to the south, have started to move northward on the return portion of their long migration move back to the tundra. First come the cows, those pregnant as a result of unions with bulls on the southward march of the previous autumn, now filled out with calf; the bulls follow far behind. Caribou in their thousands flow over the land heading north, diverted from their path only by exceptionally deep snow or by a particularly bad storm. Five or six miles an hour is their speed; thirty miles a day their average move. The herds follow traditional routes, land deeply grooved along its surface with meandering, parallel paths worn deep into the turf and soil by constant pounding of thousands of hoofs, year after year. In the spring the caribou often travel over the frozen surfaces of the lakes and rivers, in the summer they tend to follow the heights of land, crossing rivers and lakes at the same places every year. Along the way many die of accidents; drowned by waves from high winds on the lakes, swept over rapids and waterfalls on the rivers, of broken legs suffered running among the rocks trying to escape from wolves.

Early in June the lakes and rivers of the mainland tundra are beginning to break up and the caribou are nearing their summer calving grounds. The herds split up, pregnant cows scatter far and wide over the hills, the remainder to browse on the new forage of the river valleys and the lake shores. By mid-June most of the calves have been born and by the end of the month the herds have come together again—bulls, cows, yearlings, new calves, to wander for the rest of the summer wherever wind, weather, mosquitoes and food supply may take them.

In August a new restlessness comes over the herds; they usually break up into smaller groups, sometimes making a brief

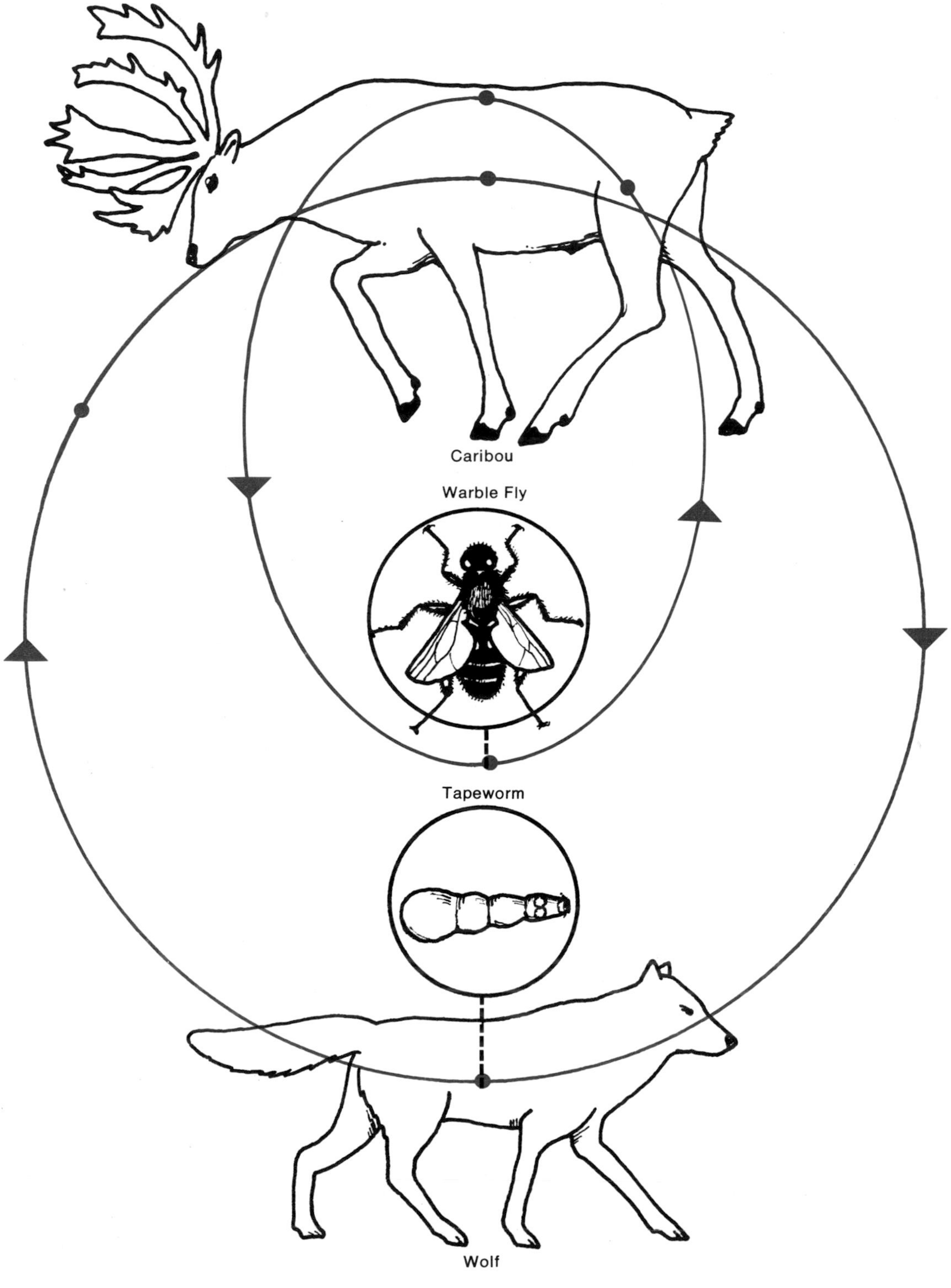

TWO MAJOR PARASITES — SCOURGE OF THE CARIBOU

In the summer months, warble flies deposit their eggs in the rump of a caribou; the eggs develop into larvae and work their way up the animal's back by burrowing under the skin. Once there, as many as 350 can feed and grow over the winter. They burrow back out and drop to the ground the following summer, to pupate and emerge as warble flies. A tapeworm begins life as a tiny egg, deposited in the intestines of a wolf, fox or dog. The eggs are later dropped in the faeces of the host animal, and may then be picked up and ingested by a browsing caribou. Once inside the caribou, they are hatched into larvae and migrate to other parts of the body where they form into cysts; in the brain or lungs such cysts can bring death to the caribou. The illustration points out the continuing cycle of these parasitic life forms.

Caribou

Warble Fly

Tapeworm

Wolf

dash southward into the edge-of-the-tree country and then back out onto the tundra again. The first sign of approaching winter and the groups come together and drift southward, gradually gathering together into great herds. By the end of September the bulls are sparring with one another in preparation for the mid-October rut; by the first week in November the rut is over and the scrawny, depleted bulls leave the females and gather into separate herds shedding their horns as they move. All during this time there has been much fighting and erratic movement of the individuals, but the main southward movement of the herds has continued. By December the main herds are feeding in the northern bush; behind they have left the smaller groups to winter on the open tundra.

In their ceaseless flow of movement north and south across the immense length and breadth of their tundra range the caribou have not been alone. Travelling with the herds have been groups of tundra wolves, the "villains" of the world of nature in the tundra biome. Tundra wolves are usually off-white or light grey in colour as opposed to the darker grey of the timber wolves to the south. On the winter feeding grounds in the bush the timber wolves have moved with the caribou herds but they rarely penetrate far onto the open tundra with the herds in the spring. The tundra wolves remain north of the tree line all winter, feeding on the herds of caribou left behind, on the musk ox, on the ground squirrels and lemmings if they cannot get caribou. These huge, white wolves are well adapted to the life of a carnivore in the tundra biome; they are big animals, weighing in at 125 pounds and more; long-legged for fast movement across the open plains; deep-chested for staying power when they have to travel fast and far; big-footed for superb traction on the chase over the snow. Their heavy coat of long, off-white fur provides ample protection from the cold wind and low temperature. The tundra wolf is a predator, superbly designed and built for its task.

Wolves kill caribou; however, the wolf hardly seems deserving of its image as a bloodthirsty killer, bent on the destruction of all wildlife in its area. The wolf usually operates as a deadly, efficient meat-gathering machine; along with the caribou it has existed on the wide range of the tundra for centuries past. Caribou eat vegetation; wolves eat caribou; a simple food chain. Many biologists consider that the wolf assists the caribou by helping keep their numbers in balance, eliminating possible overgrazing of the range. By killing off diseased and inferior animals from the herd, the wolf assists it to maintain group health and alertness, allowing no degenerative units to survive. At times wolves do kill more caribou than they can eat up immediately, but this usually occurs during the months of April, May and June, immediately prior to the whelping period for which the wolves need a good store of meat handy to the den in order to feed the bitch and the growing pups. It is interesting to note that the wolf bitch drops its cubs about the same time as the caribou cow drops its calf; thus both hunter and hunted are tied up in the cycle of birth at the same time, usually far distant from each other at just the time when the caribou needs most to be free of the association with the wolf. Could this be an adaptation to the realities of life in this land?

The best hunting for wolves is around the large herds of caribou as they move north and south across frozen land and lake. The wolf moves with the herd and the herd knows that the wolf, or wolves are there. So long as no overt movement is made by the wolf in the direction of the herd, peace reigns. Wolves can pass within fifty to one hundred yards of a large herd of caribou and not disturb the animals one whit. But when the wolf needs food it moves with precision and purpose. Rushing straight at the herd it will have picked out the animal it wishes to kill. Immediately the herd goes on the alert; those distant from the wolf do not move but they watch the proceedings with great care. Those closer to the wolf, but out of the line of its attack, are slightly uneasy but not terrified; they usually trot along, angling slightly outward to keep clear of a possible change in the direction of the attack. Those directly in front of the wolf are in full flight; quickly the gap between the hard driving wolf and the fleeing deer closes. The victim senses that it is the one and redoubles its efforts to escape. As the wolf moves in close, the other caribou angle away from the victim, leaving it alone in its flight. With a rush the wolf leaps for the neck or the throat; down goes the deer under the tremendous power of the hurtling wolf. In a moment the caribou is dead on the snow, throat cut and mangled, or head nearly torn from its body. The wolf enjoys its meal of raw meat; the rest of the caribou can settle down to feed in peace; the tundra food chain consisting of moss-caribou-wolf is now complete.

13 HUNTING MAN

No one knows why man, creature of warmth, first moved into the Arctic environment of the north polar region. Perhaps he was driven there by relentless pressure from new and more powerful groups of mankind emerging out of the heartland areas of Africa and Asia, until, eventually, certain groups found themselves facing out over the ice of the Asian Arctic seas. Perhaps he drifted north, after becoming adapted to life in a cold land in earlier times when the encroaching ice of the Pleistocene glaciers first inundated the hunting grounds of northern Europe and Asia, forcing certain groups of men who were reluctant to move far south away from the lands in which they had been born, into refugia along the outer edges of the ice. We do not know; we may never know. But, whatever the historical incentive may have been, the fact is that hunting man, at some point in his long development, met and successfully adapted to life in a land in which the dominant physical feature was ice—land under the control of cold.

The Arctic plants, insects, birds, and most of the mammals adapted to life in the cold through changes in their basic processes, their physical features, and their instinctual behaviour patterns. Man did none of these things; he used his brain and his hands to devise special ways of meeting the challenges imposed upon him by his world of ice. Hunting man had no heavy coat of fur; he took the coat of the caribou and from it fashioned warm clothing for his naked body, clothing so well designed and of such excellent insulating material that it has remained the best winter clothing ever produced, so far unduplicated for warmth and comfort while working and travelling in the Arctic winter. From the heavier, but more waterproof, skins of the sea mammals he made clothing that kept him warm and dry during the spring and summer as he hunted and travelled over the melting ice or on the open water of the sea. From the skins of the sea mammals he made lashings for his sleds; his summer shelters were made from sealskin, as were the coverings of his ingenious boats, the kayak and the umiak. Bone and ivory gave him materials he needed for his weapons—the special spears for the fish; the distinctive harpoons for the seals, the walrus and the small whales. From soft soapstone he carved his cooking pots, and the half-moon shaped oil lamps in which he burned the fat of the sea mammals to give him heat and light in his winter house made of sod and stone, or from blocks of snow.

Hunting man learned to use the cold of his far north land to his own advantage. The hard packed snow of the Arctic coast made an excellent building material, firm enough to be cut into building blocks with a bone knife, yet full of tiny air pockets

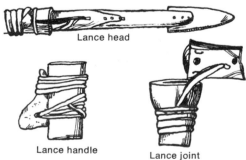

Lance head

Lance handle

Lance joint

In order to kill the elusive seal, the Eskimo hunter devised special weapons that were light enough to be wielded from his kayak, but still deadly enough to kill his prey on the first strike.

that provided excellent insulation against the severe cold. A thin film of ice on the runners of his sled made it slide more easily over the dry Arctic snow. In the central Arctic, where wood was a very scarce commodity, he often used cold to help him build his winter sled. Laying frozen Arctic char end to end and wrapping them tightly in a wet sealskin which was then allowed to freeze, he fashioned "fish and skin" plank runners for a small sled. Lashed together by skin lines and crossbars of antler or bone, such a sled could be used by one man and his family to haul their meagre possessions over the snow. It also served as an emergency food supply whenever hunting failed and he was unable to secure fresh meat.

Hunting man was the ultimate predator of the Arctic coast biome. Over land and ice and water he roamed constantly, killing in order to feed himself, his family and his dogs. Herbivorous and carnivorous, equipped with the ability to observe, to think and to reason, hunting man in the Arctic lived as a kind of super-mammal, preying on everything that came his way. He watched the caribou, studied their ways; he fashioned bows and arrows of bone and sinew to kill them and devised the techniques needed to trap them at the water crossings on the lakes and rivers, or in the long, rocky valleys that he studded with piles of rocks in imitation of men to force the caribou into the path of his primitive weapons. He made nets of sinew to trap flocks of small birds in winter; snares to catch Arctic hares;

stone traps to catch foxes and wolves; even small, stone corrals into which he would drive the flightless, moulting geese so that he could kill them with stones or clubs. He gathered eggs; he ate, and considered a great delicacy the larvae of the warble fly of the caribou.

Using his hunting kayak on the open sea he stalked and killed the swimming seals, walrus and whales with harpoons made of wood and bone and ivory. He crept up on the seals as they lay on the ice dozing in the spring sun, always in full view of the seal, moving ahead while it slept, moving about when it awoke in imitation of the seal, trying to make the seal believe that he was just another seal until he could get close enough to rush it for the kill. He hunted baby seals as they lay in their caves beneath the snow on the sea ice, breaking in the roofs of the aglos in imitation of the hunting technique of the polar bear. And for the seals under the thick ice cover, he devised an elaborate and highly successful technique for seeking out the breathing holes and harpooning the seals as they rose up to take a breath of air.

Hunting man on the Arctic coast spent his life in killing. But he was not a savage for he killed with compassion. Not the sentimental, sometimes maudlin compassion of today, but a compassion born of the belief that all the animals he killed had souls, just like himself. A man's soul was a little man; the soul of a seal was a little seal. He believed that you couldn't kill the

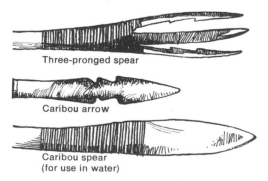

Three-pronged spear

Caribou arrow

Caribou spear
(for use in water)

Caribou provided the major source of food and clothing for inland Eskimos. The weapons illustrated above were devised by the primitive Eskimo hunter to kill the mighty animal.

Eskimo hunters killed only to meet the needs of the day as they believed the soul of a dead seal would return to seek vengeance.

soul and because of this there was great danger in the killing of all animals; once the soul was set free by the death of the body it could seek vengeance on the hunter. Especially was he vulnerable if he had failed to live up to the rules of life, the laws laid down by the wisdom of his ancestors in days long ago, the precepts we call taboos. Taboos belonged to the world of his gods who dwelt far off in the sky, beneath the land, at the bottom of the sea, in a supernatural world that was as real to the Eskimo hunter as the natural world he could see all about him.

> "Nuliakjuk, great god of mankind,
> Send us the seals,
> Send us the bears,
> Send us the walrus;
> So that we may have food
> And fat
> And clothing;
> Beasts of the sea
> Come offer yourself,
> In the cold, clear light of the morning."

The Eskimo hunter was not a conscious conservationist; sometimes he killed great numbers of caribou, far more than he could use; sometimes he blocked a river completely and fished it to near extinction, completely unaware of what was taking place. To him the thought that the animals he hunted could be killed off to extinction just did not exist; there had always been animals in his land and, despite their cyclic appearances and disappearances, they would always be there. With his primitive weapons he lacked the ability to kill on a scale grand enough to decimate animal species over their entire range; his own numbers could never grow so many as to pose a threat to the continued existence of the game on which he depended for his life, except in a short term, very local way. Besides, hunting and fishing was hard work, often dangerous work; the Eskimo hunter usually killed only to meet the needs of the day.

Today in the Arctic coast region of Canada there are a few Eskimo hunters still able to follow the mammals in the manner of their forefathers of long ago; hunters willing to wait for hours over a small hole in the winter ice, hunters able to kill caribou with bow and arrow, hunters not afraid to seek out the polar bear while armed only with the short, bone-tipped spear. Today, there are a few old people living out their lives on the shores of Chantry Inlet and Pelly Bay who still carry with them the vivid memories of their younger days, when the Eskimo hunter reigned supreme, the virtual ruler of all this far northern land.

Virtual ruler, but not absolute. For all his skill and ingenuity in adapting to the cold climate of his Arctic land, the Eskimo hunter remained a predatory mammal, one link in a simple food chain, condemned to spend his life locked into an unchanging cycle of movement from hunting area to hunting area, a tyranny of timetable even more rigid than the tyranny of the time-clock and punch-card of today. At the peak of its development his culture was a bone and stone society, locked irrevocably into a pattern of alternate feast and famine, the basic cycle of scarcity and plenty of an Arctic land. The hunter was totally dependent on the mammals of land and sea; so long as they fell beneath his spears and arrows and harpoons, he remained happy and well fed, able to live and travel throughout his land. But, when they died off, or disappeared from his area, when the herds of caribou failed to come to the water crossings; when the seals failed to come to the breathing holes; when the fish failed to swim up the rivers in the fall, then hunting man died; died of starvation and cold in the vast white emptiness of his wilderness home. His folk tales tell of such horror on the land.

"One winter, many years ago, hunting was a failure and nobody had anything to eat. People died of hunger, and the quick lived on the dead. Day after day the few remaining hunters stood over the few seal holes they were able to find by themselves, for their dogs had long since been eaten. But the seals had gone, no one knew where. Hour after hour the hunters waited, with their bellies empty and the cold pecking at their bones. Back at their snow houses they knew that their families were dying, slowly, first the old people, then the very young, then the healthy ones. Without food, without heat, without light, their lives flickered and were gone."

Such was the fortune of the high Arctic hunter—to live or to die, always unto himself, making no mark, leaving almost no record that he once passed this way. He lived in harmony and in balance with his Arctic environment, but such harmony had its dreadful price. Often he was called upon to pay.

14 THE DESTROYERS

For thousands of years the Arctic coast of Canada was known only to the primitive humans from Asia who had spread in successive waves across the top of North America, and on into Greenland. Around 1000 A.D. the early Norse began to settle the west coast of Greenland and make voyages to Baffin Island, but all records of these voyages were lost to Europe until recent times when contact between Europe and Greenland was cut off late in the fourteenth century. As recently as five hundred years ago darkness shrouded European knowledge of the Arctic world that lay beyond the vast expanse of the north Atlantic Ocean. Out beyond that shadowy horizon lay unknown lands "wherein nature breeds perverse, all monstrous, all prodigious things, worse than fables yet conceived, gorgons, Hydras, and chimeras dire, all peopled with strange infidels whose like was never seen, read nor heard before."

It wasn't until the beginning of the fifteenth century that the darkness began to lift. In quick succession came the rediscovery of the earth as a sphere; came the development of sailing vessels capable of traversing the open ocean far from land; came the discovery of the miracle of the magnetic compass. The eyes of Europe turned westward, seeking new routes to the enchanted land of Cathay—Cathay, described by Marco Polo as a form of Christian Heaven, where highways were paved in gold; a land of incense and perfume, and enough rare spices and herbs to whet the greed of every man.

Instead of Cathay western man came to the shores of northern North America, and the Arctic coast appeared to him in a much different light than it had to the earlier migrants from the east. The newcomers were as fearful of the strange land they found as they were of the fires of Hell. The "civilized" Europeans were disgusted with the primitive Eskimo, " a brutish people . . . link between Saxons and seals—hybrids, putting the seal's body into their own and then encasing their skins in the seals'." They were terrified of the winter darkness, "dark, dark, dark . . . without all hope of day." They lived in fear of the power of the ice on the sea. "No water was to be seen around our ship . . . from day to day we hoped for the hour of our deliverance; at first we expected it hourly, then daily, then from week to week, then after the seasons of the year, then at the changes in the new year. But, alas, that hour never came, never again were we destined to see our vessel in water; we were prisoners of the pack." They were awestruck by the bleak, treeless, and seemingly lifeless land under their feet, "snow and rock and broken ice surrounded us on every side. A more desolate place could not be found on earth than the land we walked on." Even today, in mid-twentieth century, with very few exceptions Canadians are afraid of their Arctic coast region; only about one tenth of one percent of Canada's population lives there, and of this miniscule proportion it is quite probable that at least one-third would rather be anywhere but where they are.

The early explorers were sea captains, hired by the businessmen of Europe to seek out new trade routes along which they could conduct their enormously profitable trade in spices, incense and jewels with the countries of the Far East. These men neither expected nor desired to find new lands between them and their goal, but when land was found they moved quickly to exploit any wealth it might contain.

The first of the European sea captains to penetrate the eastern Arctic was Martin Frobisher who, outbound from England in 1576 in his tiny ship the *Gabriel,* came to the shores of southern Baffin Island and sailed into his bay. For Frobisher the discovery of the Northwest Passage to the Orient was "the only thing of the world left undone whereby a notable mind might be made famous and fortunate." He made three voyages to the bay that now bears his name, sponsored by the newly formed Cathay Company, favoured by the interest and financial support of Queen Elizabeth who called the new land *Meta Incognita* – worth unknown – a somewhat prophetic name in view of future events. Although Frobisher started out to find a passage to the Orient he was diverted from his task by a chance discovery. "The Captain and six of his men landed on a small island where they found many strange flowers and grasses among the stones . . . one of the men found a piece of black stone by the weight of which seemed to be some kind of metal or mineral . . . they came to a place where all the sands and rocks did glisten so that all seemed to be gold."

Gold! The quest for the Northwest Passage was all but forgotten. "Upon this island was found a good store of the ore,

whereupon it was thought best to load here than to seek further. Setting the miners to work, our Captain showed a good precedent of painful labour himself, whereupon every man, both better and worse, willingly laid their helping hands . . . with the hold of the ship full of ore we set sail for home."

Alas! Frobisher's gold turned out to be iron pyrites. The Cathay Company was bankrupt; the ore so laboriously hauled across the Atlantic was dumped into the harbour at Bristol, England, where four hundred years later it would cause considerable damage to a dredge working at deepening the harbour. Northern North America's first mine came into production in the Arctic coast region of Canada; its open pit scars the landscape of Kadloonak Island today.

Very quickly did the merchants of western Europe adapt to the newly discovered facts about the geography and natural history of the Arctic coasts of the world. Out from the sea ports of Spain, France, Holland and England came huge fleets of whaling vessels, hundreds of ships employing thousands of men, all seeking the great whales that swam in uncounted numbers in the waters off the Arctic coasts; the huge Greenland "right" whale, its body larded with tons of blubber that could be rendered down into oil for the lamps of Europe and Asia, its mouth a mass of thin, parallel plates of baleen, a unique substance in the animal world, light, tough and flexible, able to be split along its entire length into strips of any desired thinness, ideal material to help shape the form and figure of the ladies of the courts at St. James and The Hague; and the sperm whale, equally well-laden with blubber, without baleen but having in its massive head an enormous reservoir of spermaceti, basis for cosmetics and perfumes. In the seventeenth century, whales from Arctic waters lighted Europe, greased its wheels, provided its soap, and kept its ladies in trim.

As the prices for whale oil and baleen increased – in 1775 the products from a single whale brought about $3,000 at the port of Dundee but by the early 1900's this had increased to as much as $10,000 per whale – whaling became one of the biggest extractive industries of the western world. It brought fortunes to many and, in the disputes it generated, it brought nations to the brink of war. The risks of whaling were high; between 1772 and 1852 eighty ships from a single port were lost at sea or crushed in the ice. On a single day, June 19th, 1830, nineteen

WHALERS – LONG THE SCOURGE OF THE ARCTIC SEAS

In the three hundred years between 1600 and 1900 the Arctic whales were hunted relentlessly by vast fleets of ships. The voyages often lasted three years and the conditions on board these ships were so incredibly harsh that they provided material for several novels on the nineteenth century. The whales provided lamp oil, axel grease, soap and whalebone for Europe and North America. The illustration depicts the normal whaling operation during this bloody period.

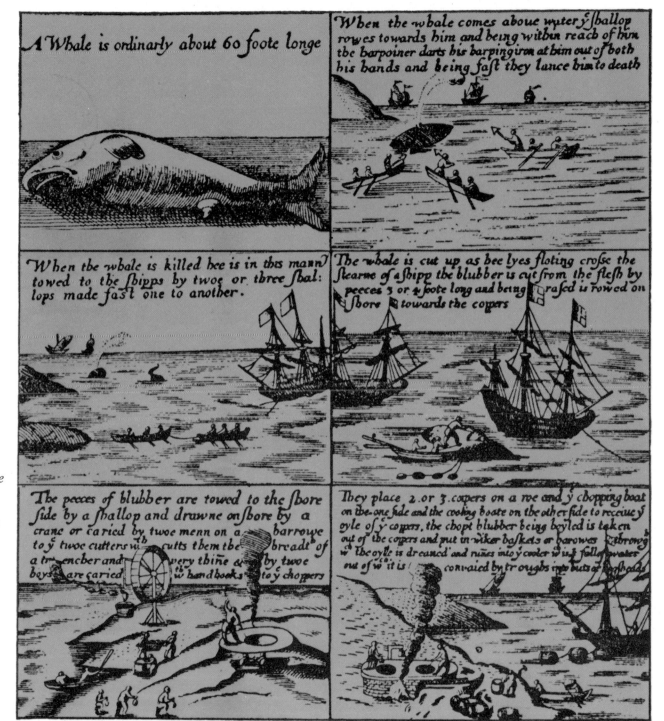

A Whale is ordinarly about 60 foote longe

When the whale comes aboue wyter ý shallop rowes towards him and being within reach of him the harpoiner darts his harpingiron at him out of both his hands and being fast they lance him to death

When the whale is killed hee is in this manñ towed to the shipps by twoe or three shal: lops made fast one to another.

The whale is cut up as hee lyes floting crosse the stearne of a shipp the blubber is cut from the flesh by peeces 3 or 4 foote long and being rased is rowed on shore towards the copers

The peeces of blubber are towed to the shore side by a shallop and drawne onshore by a crane or caried by twoe menn on a barrowe to ý twoe cutters w:th cutts them the breadt of a trencher and very thiñe & by twoe boys are caried w:th handhooks into ý choppers

They place 2. or 3. copers on a roe and ý chopping boat on the one side and the cooking boate on the other side to receiue ý oyle of ý copers, the chopt blubber being boyled is taken out of the copers and put in wiker baskets or barowes w:th strong w:th the oyle is dreaned and runes into ý cooler w:th full of water out of w:th it is conuaied by troughs into buts of

137

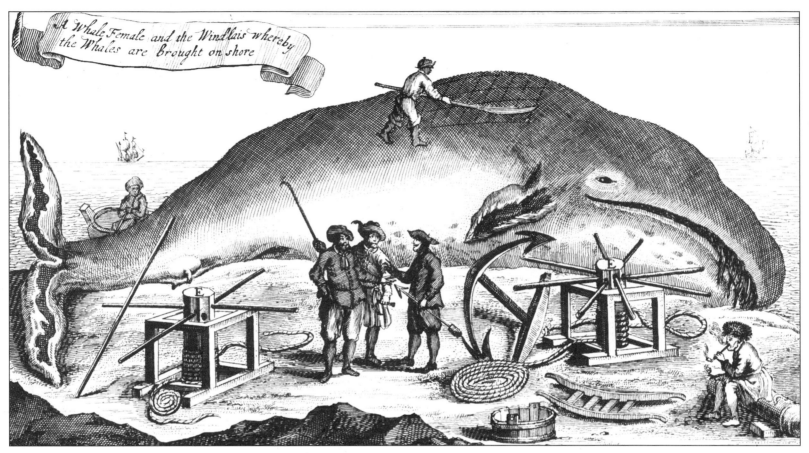

No one questioned the wisdom of destroying so valuable a source of oil, baleen and spermaceti, so long as sale profits kept pouring in.

ships of the Hull whaling fleet were crushed against the land-fast floe and destroyed, leaving over one thousand men stranded on the sea ice of Melville Bay. But, high as the risks were, the chance of profit was even higher; there was rarely a shortage of money to outfit new vessels, nor a shortage of men to act as their eager crews.

Little has been written about this black period in the history of men on the sea. Arctic waters were far from the centres of civilization; the high seas were anyone's domain. So long as the oil and the baleen and the spermaceti poured into the warehouses, and the profits from their sale poured into the pockets of seamen, merchants and princes alike, no one questioned the ultimate wisdom of destroying so valuable a resource of the

open sea. Out of sight, out of mind, seemed to have been the order of the day.

For over three hundred years the whalers were the scourge of the Arctic seas. Through the seventeenth century they destroyed the herds of whales in the coastal waters of the Greenland and Norwegian Seas. By the eighteenth century dwindling catches along the coast forced them onto the open sea where they killed whales with relentless ferocity. Following hard on the heels of the explorers, in cases even preceding them, they moved into the more distant waters of Davis Strait and Baffin Bay, into the inlets of the eastern Arctic islands, until, by the late nineteenth and early twentieth century, they had penetrated deep into Hudson Bay. In the west they moved north from the

Great numbers of walrus were also included in the indiscriminate destruction by the whalers, who expected to profit by the ivory tusks.

Pacific through Bering Strait into the Chukchee and Beaufort Seas. Early in the twentieth century, from the whaling base at Herschel Island, American whalers hunted the big whales as far east as the waters of Amundsen Gulf and north into the Arctic Ocean. Until the invention of substitutes for whalebone in the year 1906, which brought about the complete collapse of the whaling industry in northern waters in the space of a single year, the whaler was despotic king of the Arctic seas.

No one knows the numbers of whales destroyed through three centuries of unrestricted killing; the total count would probably stagger the imagination. So many were killed that the large whales virtually disappeared from Arctic waters; where they once swam and fed and blew in their hundreds, they appear now only rarely, usually as single animals, at most two or three. It is quite likely that the large whales are gone forever from the waters of the Arctic coast region of Canada, too few in number to perpetuate their kind.

The destructiveness of the whalers did not end with the killing off of the whales. They also killed great numbers of walrus and polar bears; walrus for their ivory tusks, polar bears for their luxuriant white coats, both valuable items of trade in the marketplaces of Europe and Asia. And, at their wintering-over places on the Arctic coasts, at Fullerton on the northwest coast of Hudson Bay, at Herschel Island off the mouth of the Mackenzie, at various locations on the east coast of Baffin Island, the whalers hunted out over the land, or encouraged the local Eskimos to hunt for them, killing thousands upon thousands of caribou, hundreds of musk ox to keep themselves supplied with fresh meat. As with the whales in the sea, no one knows how many animals were slaughtered over the years but the total number must have been as equally enormous as those butchered on the sea.

"One winter fifteen vessels wintered at Herschel Island and I am reliably informed that these vessels each used from 10,000 to 20,000 pounds of caribou meat an aggregate of over 300,000 pounds in one winter, principally the saddles; at the head of Franklin Bay, in the winter of 1897-98, four ships used of the same kind of meat about 90,000 pounds, and at Cape Bathurst, in 1898-99, one vessel used in the neighbourhood of 40,000 pounds." Small wonder that a government report, compiled long after the whaling ships and their rapacious crews had passed from the scene, concluded that "the whaling fleet at the commencement of this century was a primary factor in the serious reduction of these herds (of caribou) along the western Arctic coast."

For thousands of years life in the tundra biome of North America, and in the waters and on the ice of the seas along the Arctic coasts, had co-existed within a stable ecological unit that embraced within its borders a delicately balanced world of plants and animals, including hunting man, all especially adapted to life in a land under the control of cold. Then, in the short space of three hundred years, this world was shattered and laid waste by the predations of western man, creature of warmth, moving as an itinerant visitor and intruder into what he considered to be a disordered land. The early explorers ended the isolation of the Arctic coast from the rest of the world; the whalers followed, first to systematically kill off much of the big game of land and sea, then to become dealers in ivory and fur. For when whaling died many whalers remained on the Arctic coast as independent traders. Both as whalers and traders they encouraged the local Eskimo groups to change their way of life from that of a free-roaming hunter, intent only on obtaining food for himself and his family, into that of a hunt-and-trap-for-profit businessman who killed caribou and musk ox for sale to the ships' crews; who killed polar bears, foxes and wolves for their fur, walrus and small whales for their ivory, all of which he traded for rifles and ammunition, pots and pans, clothing of wool and cotton, trinkets of glass and brass, all items that

The harsh natural environment frequently took its revenge on the rapacious whaling fleets.

only added weight to his equipment and nothing at all to his ability to survive as a hunter in a cold land.

Whalers of the seventeenth and eighteenth centuries were at least partly responsible for the disappearance of the Thule Eskimo culture for, although change in Arctic coast climate was undoubtedly a basic factor in the dwindling away of the Thule culture from the north coast of Canada, the killing off of the large whales probably contributed much to the destruction of this advanced hunting society; even without the increasing severity of the weather the slaughter of the big whales would have eventually brought about its demise. There is no doubt that the whalers destroyed, or at least planted the seed that would destroy, the society of the modern Eskimo hunter of the Arctic coast; directly by killing off groups of people through strange diseases they introduced, indirectly by so changing the mores and habits and thinking of the remaining indigenous inhabitants that a high Arctic culture, the like of which the world will never see again, began to slip away into oblivion in a process that has continued unabated down through the first half of the present century, and continues in its last stages today.

The whalers of the Arctic coast have passed into history; the last of the Arctic hunters will very soon be but a memory as western technology moves ever deeper into the Arctic coast region. On the land, herds of caribou still roam the tundra, much reduced in numbers and haunted by the spectre of extinction through excessive predation, disease, reduction of range due to fire, poor calf crops due to inclement weather at calving time, but still a viable element of the tundra biome that, with good management and some luck, will survive and thrive in future generations. Musk ox, now completely protected, are increasing in numbers after being nearly wiped out through excessive killing by explorers, whalers and Eskimos alike. In the sea the big whales are nearly gone, but seals and walrus still swim along the coasts or sleep on the ice in the spring sun, polar bears still roam the icefields, all being killed in ever-increasing numbers but being studied and watched so that it is quite probable that their future well being is assured. And, although we western humans still tend to look upon the Arctic as a distant land of ice and snow, we are beginning to study it, to learn from it, to adapt our technology to its unique conditions.

But we cannot be complacent about the future in the natural

Western culture has almost destroyed the native way of life.

history of the Arctic coast region. Although any repeat of the mass slaughter of earlier years is unlikely, the Arctic is still a long way from southern Canada; what goes on there often seems to be quite remote, quite separate from life in the south. In today's world nothing could be further from the truth. The world has become a global village in which all events concern all peoples, no matter where they may be. Nowhere is this better illustrated than by what some scientists have come to call "the new caribou problem."

Lichens stand at the bottom of an Arctic food chain, deriving their sustenance from the sun and from the fall-out of natural materials in the air. Until the explosion of the first atomic bomb in 1945 lichens absorbed only the harmless fall-out of dust and other wind-blown materials; today they absorb the radioactive fall-out resulting from the nuclear explosions in the atmosphere of the world. Lichens are extremely efficient garnerers of materials from the air and they grow very slowly, storing up in their exposed, edible parts the fall-out particles of many years. Over the years lichens of the Arctic coasts have built up a high degree of radioactive contamination.

Caribou eat lichens, commonly called caribou moss, as a primary food and, as a result, caribou (and reindeer) of Canada, Alaska, Scandinavia and Russia have begun to show excessive levels of contamination by radioactive elements, principally Strontium-90 and Cesium-137. In some cases the levels are far above that recommended as being "safe" for man. On the Arctic coasts man eats caribou meat, often as a primary food. Although data is scarce as yet, what little there is seems to indicate that radioactive contamination of humans feeding on caribou and reindeer meat is much higher than that in humans feeding on other meats. Thus it would seem that the entire food chain of lichen-caribou-man, in sections of the Arctic coast regions of the world, is becoming excessively contaminated by radioactive materials.

This problem was first noted in 1959; since that time there has been little additional research and almost no publicity. Yet it is a problem that affects all life in an area that comprises almost one third of Canada; on the world stage it affects an area that makes up almost one-fifth of the land in the northern hemisphere. There is little doubt that if a similar situation existed in southern Canada, in the grass-cattle-man food chain,

reaction would be immediate and violent. But the Arctic coast is a long way off, lichens are an unfamiliar plant, the caribou is a strange animal. Except to a few scientists the problems of the lichen-caribou-man food chain seem no closer to most of us today than did the problem of the whales seem to the average man and woman of the eighteenth century.

This thinking must change. Here in Canada we have gone from a stage of not thinking about our Arctic at all to a situation in which we think about it quite a bit, but usually in the romantic sense—the land of the Eskimo, of Eskimo art, the true north strong and free. Or we think about it in the economic sense; we talk about oil and gas beneath the land of the high Arctic islands, copper, iron and nickel under the rocks of the Shield. We see visions of northern development, with new mines, new towns, new people with new thoughts building new empires out beyond the northerly limit of the trees. And so we should, for we are Canadians; our land stretches north to within some 450 miles of the true North Pole.

But as we dream our northern dreams we should remember that, even with the most optimistic development of the resources beneath the land, we would still be utilizing only a tiny fraction of the land area of the tundra biome. Our new mines and town-sites and airfields would be but pin-pricks on this vast land. All about would still be the enormous areas of land and sea on and in which live the cold-adapted plants, insects, birds, mammals, each one a resource, each one tied inextricably into a basic food chain of an Arctic land, each slow to grow and slow to reproduce, and thus easily destroyed if the system is thrown out of kilter by unmanaged, exploitive use of one or more elements in the vital chain.

Remote from the rest of Canada, sparse in human population, meagrely represented in the power structure of government, the natural world of the Arctic coast must rely for its future well-being on the continuing interest of science, on the understanding and vociferous pleading of a special few, and, ultimately, on the understanding and co-operation of millions of people in southern Canada who will never see the Arctic, who will always consider it to be a disordered land, but who care enough about all parts of their country to make sure that the Arctic coast will remain forever as a living symbol of the great wilderness that was once our entire world.

GEOLOGIC TIME SCALE

TIME	ERA	PERIOD	EPOCH	THE ASCENT OF LIFE:
	CENOZOIC	QUATERNARY	PLEISTOCENE	
		TERTIARY	PLIOCENE	
			MIOCENE	
			OLIGOCENE	
50			EOCENE	
			PALEOCENE	
100	MESOZOIC	CRETACEOUS	UPPER	
			LOWER	
150		JURASSIC	UPPER MIDDLE LOWER	
200		TRIASSIC	UPPER MIDDLE LOWER	
250	PALAEOZOIC	PERMIAN	UPPER MIDDLE LOWER	
300		PENNSYLVANIAN		
350		MISSISSIPPIAN		
		DEVONIAN	UPPER MIDDLE LOWER	
400		SILURIAN		
450		ORDOVICIAN	UPPER MIDDLE LOWER	
500				
550		CAMBRIAN	UPPER MIDDLE LOWER	

MILLIONS OF YEARS

THE ASCENT OF LIFE: 1, *protozoan*;   2, *jellyfish*;   3, *crinoid*;   4, *cephalopod*;   5, *climatius*;   6, *shark*;   7, *brachiopod*;   8, *seed fern*;   9, *dimetrodon*;   10, *brontosaurus*;   11, *plesiosaur*;   12, *tyrannosaurus*;   13, *taeniolabis*;   14, *diatryma*;   15, *hyracotherium*;   16, *brontotherium*;   17, *oxydactylus*;   18, *pliohippus*;   19, *mastodon*;   20, *man*.

143

SHORT LIST OF ROCKS, PLANTS AND ANIMALS

The lists on the following pages have been compiled as a basic guide for amateur naturalists intending to explore the wealth of natural history of the Arctic Coast region. These selected summaries cannot possibly cover all species — there are many thousands of insects alone — but an attempt has been made to include the common life forms and the natural phenomena peculiar to this region. Readers should find it useful to study the lists touching on their sphere of interest, checking off items they have observed during field trips. Those wishing to extend their search will find an extensive Bibliography on pages 153-5; references listed there contain more detailed information on specific subjects.

ROCKS

CENOZOIC ERA

TERTIARY PERIOD
Carbonized wood
Gypsum
Lignite
Mudstone
Sand
Sandstone
Shale

MESOZOIC ERA

CRETACEOUS PERIOD
Black shale
Clay
Coal
Diabase
Ironstone
Sandstone
Shale
Siltstone
Volcanic breccia

JURASSIC PERIOD
Coal
Conglomerate
Dolomite
Phosphatic nodules
Sand
Sandstone
Shale

TRIASSIC PERIOD
Limestone
Sandstone
Siltstone
Shale

PALAEOZOIC ERA

MISSISSIPPIAN AND PENNSYLVANIA PERIOD
Basalt
Chert
Conglomerate
Greywacke
Gypsum
Lignite
Limestone
Phyllite
Sandstone
Shale
Siltstone
Tuff

DEVONIAN PERIOD
Coal
Conglomerate
Coralline Limestone
Dolomite
Sandstone
Sandy shale
Siltstone
Slate

SILURIAN PERIOD
Argillite
Black limestone
Black shale
Gypsum
Mudstone
Sandstone

ORDOVICIAN PERIOD
Anhydrite
Dolomite
Gypsum
Limestone
Sandstone
Shale

CAMBRIAN PERIOD
Dolomite
Gypsum
Limestone
Sandstone

PRECAMBRIAN ERA
Argillite
Dolomite
Gneisses
Greenstone
Limestone
Marble
Paragneiss
Quartzite
Quartz-mica schist
Sandstone
Shale
Siltstone
Slate

MINERALS

The minerals listed are those most likely to be found in the regions named.

BAFFIN ISLAND
Allanite
Antimony
Apatite
Asbestos
Coal
Cobalt
Columbite
Copper
Cordierite

Diopside
Fluorite
Garnet
Graphite
Gypsum
Hematite
Iron
Lapis Lazuli
Lazurite
Magnetite
Marble
Mica
Native sulphur
Nickel
Phosphorous
Platinum
Pyrite
Quartz
Scapolite
Serpentine
Sillimanite
Silver
Soapstone
Spinel
Steatite
Tourmaline

MACKENZIE DISTRICT
Chromite
Cobalt
Copper
Gold
Nickel
Pentlandite
Pitchblende
Silver
Soapstone
Sphalerite

HIGH ARCTIC ISLANDS DISTRICT
Agate
Chalcedony
Copper
Jasper
Pentlandite
Sphalerite

KEEWATIN DISTRICT
Amethyst
Arsenic
Chalcopyrite
Chromite bearing minerals
Copper
Fluorite
Gold
Jasper
Molybdenite

Pentlandite
Pitchblende
Platinum
Pyrite
Pyrrhotite
Quartz
Silver

WESTERN ARCTIC ISLANDS
Copper
Pyrite
Serpentine

UNGAVA
Asbestos
Chalcopyrite
Copper
Galena
Garnet
Graphite
Hematite
Iron
Jasper
Jaspilite
Magnetite
Pyrite
Pyrrhotite
Quartz
Silver
Soapstone

FOSSILS

Southern Baffin Island
SILURIAN
Corals
Calapoecia borealis
Halysites catenularia
Halysites catenulatus
Heliolites megastoma
Gastropods
Loxonema sp.
Hormotoma sp.
Lophospira sp.
Cephalopods
Endoceras sp.
Cyrtoceras sp.
Huronia sp.

ORDOVICIAN
Stromatoporoids
Stromatocerium
Corals
Calapoecia anticostiensis
Zaphrentis sp.

Gastropods
Maclurites sp.
Lophospira sp.
Eotomaria sp.
Cephalopods
Armenoceras richardsoni
Endoceras proteiforme
Actinceras sp.
Trocholites ammonius
Trilobites
Ogygites canadensis

*Grinnell Peninsula
(Devon Island)*
PERMIAN
Foraminifera
Schubertella kingi
Pseudofusulinella utahensis
Schwagerina paralinearis
Corals
Caninia ovibos
Lithostrotion grandis
Roemeripora wimani
Brachiopods
Lingula arctica
Streptorhynchus kempei
Muirwoodia mammatus
Stenoscisma plicatum
Cephalopods
Pseudogastrioceras fortieri
Metalegoceras sp.

*Banks, Victoria and
Stefansson Islands*
CRETACEOUS
Plankton
Cyclonocephalum distinctum
Deflandrea acuminata
Hystrichosphaeridium complex
Pelecypods
Nucula athabaskensis
Psilomya elongatissima
Beudanticeras affine
Arctica limpidiana
DEVONIAN
Foraminifera
Schubertella sp.
Brachiopods
Gypidula pseudogaleata
Nervostrophia sp.
Pelecypods
Paracyclas robusta

SILURIAN
Corals
Favosites sp.
Syringopora sp.
Brachiopods
Atrypella scheii

ORDOVICIAN
Corals
Receptaculites sp.
Cephalopods
Gonioceras sp.
Brachiopods
Pholidops trentonensis

Ellesmere Islands
TERTIARY
Ferns
Lycopodium sp.
Laevigatosporites albertensis
Gleichenia concavisporites
Osmundacidites primarius
Gleichenia concavisporites
Conifers
Pinus strobipites
Picea grandivescipites
Taxodium hiatipites
Larix sp.
Angiosperms
Betula sp.
Corylus sp.
Carya sp.
Myrica sp.

LOWER AND MIDDLE ORDOVICIAN
Gastropods
Liospira sp.
Hormotoma sp.
Turritoma sp.
Cephalopods
Spyroceras sp.
Gonioceras sp.
Trilobites
Bathyurus sp.
Isotelus sp.

LOWER ORDOVICIAN
Brachiopods
Lingulella sp.
Cephalopods
Euconia quebecensis
Clarkoceras holtedahli
Trilobites
Hystricurus ravni
Hystricurus longicephalus

MIDDLE CAMBRIAN

Trilobites
Glossopleura expansa
Glossopleura longifrons
Glossopleura walcotti
Clavaspidella sp.

LOWER CAMBRIAN

Brachiopods
Acrothele pulchra
Trilobites
Paedeumias borealis
Bonniopsis rostrata
Bonniopsis nasuta

Western Queen Elizabeth Islands

TERTIARY

Tree pollen
Pine
Spruce
Hemlock
Birch
Alder
Hazel
Poplar

CRETACEOUS

Plant microfossils
Alisporites
Abietaepollenites
Gleicheniidites
Stenozonotriletites
Ammonites
Beudanticeras affine
Lemuroceras belli

UPPER JURASSIC

Pelecypods
Buchia piochii
Buchia fischeri
Buchia blandfordiana
Buchia bronni
Buchia keyserlingi
Vertebrates
Plesiosaur
Elasmosaur
Ichthyosaur

PERMIAN

Pelecypods
Plicatula hekiensis
Gryphaea arcuatiformis
Monotis ochotica
Protocardia striatula

Cephalopods
Dactylioceras commune

PENNSYLVANIAN

Corals
Chaetetes radians
Brachiopods
Muirwoodia mammatus
Linproductus cora
Echinoconcus punctatus
Productus longispinus
Choristites fritschi
Diclyoclostus gruenewaldti
Streptorhynchus kempei

DEVONIAN

Corals
Spongophyllum sp.
Cystiphylloides sp.
Disphyllum sp.
Brachiopods
Atrypa independensis
Reticularia curvata
Lingula melvillensis
Camarotoechia lettiensis
Schizophoria sp.
Pelecypods
Nuculana sp.
Cephalopods
Bactrites sp.
Crustaceans
Estheria canadensis
Fish
Bothriolepis sp.

SILURIAN

Brachiopods
Atrypa reticularis
Gastropods
Styliolina sp.
Tentaculites sp.

ORDOVICIAN

Graptolites
Tetragraptus quadribrachiatus
Didymograptus extensus
Didymograptus uniformis
Isograptus gibberulus
Climacograptus bicornis
Petalograptus palmeus
Monograptus regularis
Corals
Coenites sp.
Brachiopods
Conchidium alaskense

PLANTS

LICHENS

Polyblastia hyperborea
Sphaerophorus globosus
Placynthium asperellum
Psoroma hypnorum
Solorina crocea
Nephroma arcticum
Peltigera aphthosa
Peltigera scabrosa
Lecidea melinodes
Lecidea tesselata
Lecidea dicksonii
Rhizocarpon chionophilum
Rhizocarpon jemtlandicum

Reindeer moss
Cladonia pyxidata
Cladonia alpestris
Cladonia rangiferina
Cladonia mitis
Cladonia bellidiflora
Cladonia unicialis
Shrubby lichen
Stereocaulon alpinum
Stereocaulon arcticum
Omphalodiscus virginis
Gyrophora proboscidea
Gyrophora hyperborea
Gyrophora arctica
Sporostatia testudinea
Pertusaria oculata
Pertusaria coriabea
Lecanora epibryon
Lecanora verrucosa
Haematomma ventosum
Skull lichen
Parmelia saxatilis
Iceland moss
Cetraria islandica
Cetraria nivalis
Cetraria cucullata
Dactylina arctica
Dactylina ramulosa
Cornicularia divergens

Rock tripe
Rinodina roscida
Physcia musigena
Thamnolia vermicularis

MOSSES

Sphagnum songstromii
Sphagnum capillaceum
Andreaea rupestris
Fissidens exiguus
Ditrichum flexicaule

Horn-tooth moss
Ceratodon purpureus
Distichium capillaceum
Wind-blown moss
Dicranum elongatum
Dicranum groenlandicum
Dicranum fuscescens
Extinguisher moss
Encalypta rhabdocarpa
Tortella fragilis
Didymodon recurvirostris
Pottia heimii
Tortula ruralis
Grimmia apocarpa
Rhacomitrium lanuginosum
Tetraplodon mnioides
Hapladon wormskjoldii
Pohlia cruda
Pohlia nutans
Leptorbryum pyriforma
Hair cap moss
Polytrichum alpinum
Bryum pendulum
Bryum obtusifolium
Bryum calophyllum
Mnium affine
Cinclidium subrotundum
Campylium stellatum
Aulocomnium acuminatum
Meesea uliginosa
Bartramia ithyphylla
Conostomum boreale
Philonotis tomentella
Timmia austriaca
Orthotrichum speciosum
Amphidium lapponicum
Myurella apiculata
Myurella julacae
Abietinella abietina
Campylium stellatum
Drepanocladus uncinatus
Calliergon turgescens
Tomenthypnum nitens
Carpet moss
Hypnum revolutum

Stair-step moss
Hylocomium splendens

HORSETAILS

Common horsetail
Equisetum arvense

Variegated horsetail
Equisetum veriegatum

Scouring rush
Equisetum scirpoides

FERNS

Rusty woodsia
Woodsia ilvensis

Alpine woodsia
Woodsia alpina

Smooth woodsia
Woodsia glabella

Fragile bladder fern
Cystopteris fragilis

Fragrant shield fern
Dryopteris fragrans

SEDGES

Tall cotton grass
Eriophorum angustifolium

Cotton grass
Eriophorum scheuchzeri

Needle spike-rush
Eleocharis acicularis
Kobresia myosuroides
Kobresia hyperborea

RUSHES

Bog rush
Juncus castaneus
Juncus biglumis

Woodrush
Luzula wahlenbergi
Luzula nivalis

False asphodel
Tofieldia pusilla

GRASSES

Holygrass
Hierochloe odorata

Sweetgrass
Hierochloe alpina

Foxtail
Phippsia algida

Bentgrass
Agrostis borealis

Reed-bentgrass
Calamagrostis purpurascens

Hairgrass
Deschampsia pumila

Short-hairgrass
Deschampsia brevifolia

Bluegrass
Poa alpigena

Arctic bluegrass
Poa arctica

Mountain bluegrass
Poa alpina

Semaphore grass
Pleuropogon sabenei

Marshgrass
Dupontia fisheri

Goosegrass
Puccinellia angustata

Meadow-grass
Puccinellia bruggemanni
Puccinellia poacea

Sheathed meadowgrass
Puccinellia vaginata

Northern fescue
Festuca baffinensis

Wheatgrass
Agropyron latiglume

Lyme-grass
Elymus arenarius

Buckwheat
Koenigia islandica

HERBS

Alpine bistort
Polygonum viviparum

Mountain sorrel
Oxyria digyna

Arctic sourdock
Rumex arcticus

Knotweed
Polygonum viviparum

Eskimo rhubarb
Polygonum alaskanum

Purslane
Montia lamprosperma

Chickweed

Stellaria longipes
Stellaria humifusa
Stellaria crassifolia

Mouse-ear chickweed

Cerastium alpinum
Cerastium arcticum
Cerastium regelii

Pearlwort
Sagina caespitosa
Sagina nodosa
Sagina intermedia

Sea-beach sandwort
Arenaria peploides

Sandwort
Arenaria humifusa
Arenaria rubella
Arenaria rossii
Arenaria sajanensis

Moss-campion
Silene acaulis

Arctic bladder-campion
Melandrium arcticum

Common campion
Melandrium affine

Wild bladder campion
Melandrium triflorum

Marsh marigold
Caltha palustris

White water-buttercup
Ranunculus trichophyllus

Pallas' buttercup
Ranunculus pallasii

Lapland buttercup
Ranunculus lapponicus

Snow buttercup
Ranunculus nivalis

Dwarf buttercup
Ranunculus pygmaeus

Arctic poppy
Papaver radicatum
Papaver keelei

Scurvy grass
Cochlearia officinalis

Tansy mustard
Descurainia sophioides

Whitlow grass
Draba alpina
Draba belli
Draba nivalis
Draba lactea
Draba subcapitata
Draba glabella
Draba groenlandica

Bitter cress
Cardamine bellidifolia

Rock cress
Arabis arenicola

Wallflower
Erysimum pallasii
Braya arctica
Braya purpurascens

Yellow mountain saxifrage
Saxifraga aizoides

White mountain saxifrage
Saxifraga aizoon

Tufted saxifrage
Saxifraga chespitosa

Nodding saxifrage
Saxifraga cernua

Spider plant
Saxifraga flagellaris

Yellow marsh saxifrage
Saxifraga propinqua

Alpine saxifrage
Saxifraga nivalis

Purple saxifrage
Saxifraga oppositifolia

Brook saxifrage
Saxifraga rivularis

Prickly saxifrage
Saxifraga tricuspidata

Golden saxifrage
Chrysosplenium tetrandrum

Grass-of-Parnassus
Parnassia kotzebuei

Cloudberry (baked apple)
Rubus chamaemorus

Arctic cinquefoil
Potentilla hypartica

Beautiful cinquefoil
Potentilla pulchella

Cinquefoil
Potentilla rubricaulis
Potentilla vahliana

Mountain avens
Dryas integrifolia

Milk-vetch
Astragalus richardsoni

Alpine milk-vetch
Astragalus alpinus

Liquorice-root
Hedysarum alpinum

Crowberry (curlewberry)
Empetrum nigrum

Willow herb
Epilobium arcticum

Water-milfoil
Myriophyllum exalbescens

Mare's-tail
Hippuris vulgaris

Nodding wintergreen
Pyrola secunda

Large flowered wintergreen
Pyrola grandiflora

Labrador tea
Ledum decumbens

Arctic white heather
Cassiope tetragona

Lapland rosebay
Rhododendron lapponicum

Billberry
Vaccinium uliginosum

Primrose
Primula stricta

Leadwort
Armeria maritima

Jacob's ladder
Polemonium boreale

Richardson's phlox
Phlox richardsoni

Lungwort
Mertensia maritima

Lapland lousewort
Pedicularis lapponica

Labrador lousewort
Pedicularis labradorica

Woolly lousewort
Pedicularis lanata

Hairy lousewort
Pedicularis hirsuta

Butterwort
Pinguicula vulgaris

Bellflower
Campanula rotundifolia

Aster
Aster pygmaeus

Fleabane
Erigeron grandiflorus

Everlasting
Antennaria glabrata
Antennaria angustata
Antennaria ekmaniana
Antennaria compacta

Wild chamomile
Matricaria ambigua

Chrysanthemum
Chrysanthemum integrifolium

Wormwood
Artemisia hyperborea

Northern wormwood
Artemisia borealis

Richardson's wormwood
Artemisia richardsoniana

Sweet coltsfoot
Petasites frigidus

Yellow arnica
Arnica alpina

Marsh-fleabane
Senecio congestus

Dandelion
Taraxacum lacerum
Taraxacum hyparcticum
Taraxacum pumilum
Taraxacum phymatocarpum

Hawk's beard
Crepis nana

SHRUBS

WILLOWS
Wideleaf dwarf willow
Salix herbacea

Tundra dwarf willow
Salix arctophila
Salix pulchra

Richardson's willow
Salix richardsonii

Netvein dwarf willow
Salix reticulata
Salix alexensis
Salix niphoclada

Ungava willow
Salix cordifolia

Tundra birch
Betula glandulosa

Dwarf birch
Betula nana

COMMON EDIBLE PLANTS

Rock tripe (tripe-de-roche)
Gryophora

Reindeer Moss
Cladonia rangiferina
Cladonia sylvatica
Cladonia alpestris
Cetraria islandica

SEAWEED
Rhodymenia palmato
Laminaria spp.

HERBS
Lousewort
Pedicularis lanata

Arctic lousewort
Pedicularis arctica

Hairy lousewort
Pedicularis hirsuta

Fernweed
Pedicularis sudetica

Mountain sorrel
Oxyria digyna

Eskimo rhubarb
Polygonum alaskanum

Arctic sourdock
Rumex arcticus

Sweet coltsfoot
Petasites frigidus

Marsh-fleabane
Senecio congestus

Seabeach-sandwort
Arenaria peploides

Round-leaved saxifrage
Saxifrage punctata

Marsh marigold (cowslip)
Caltha palustris arctica

ROOTS
Liquorice-root
Hedysarum alpinum

Alpine bistort
Polygonum viviparum

Scurvy grass
Cochlearia officinalis

FRUITS and BERRIES
Crowberry
Empetrum nigrum

Baked apple
Rubus chamaemorus

Billberry
Vaccinium uliginosum

ANIMALS

SPIDERS
Erigone psychrophila
Pardosa glacialis
Tarantula exasperans
Xysticus deichmanni
Minyriolus pampia
Microphantidae
Collinsia spitsbergensis

Crab spider
Tegenaria destabilis

MITES
Cocceupodes curviclaua
Haemogamasus alaskensis
Laelaps alaskensis
Hirstionyssus isabellinus
Protereunetes borneri
Nanorchestes collinus
Liochthonius sellnicki
Brachychthonius scalaris
Fuscozetes sellnicki
Oribita lucasii
Tectocepheus velatus
Trichoribates polaris

Springtails
Collembola

Anurida sp.
Hypogatrura viatica
Hypogatrura humi
Agrenia bidenticulata
Folsomia bisetosa
Folsomia regularis
Folsomia diplophthalma
Folsomia fimitaria
Isotomurus palustris
Isomata viridis
Isomata violacea
Isomata olivacea
Onychiurus groenlandicus
Onychiurus debilis
Neelus minimum
Sminthurides malmgrini
Sminthurides aquaticus
Archisotoma besselsi
Neogastrura tullbergi
Proisotama mackenziana

INSECTS
Aphids
Homoptera
Mealybug
Pseudococcus (trionymus) sp.
Caddis fly
Apatania zonella

MOTHS and BUTTERFLIES
Tussock moth
Gynaephora rossi
Plusia moth
Syngrapha parilis
Tiger moth
Parasemia parthenos
Looper moth
Pheumaptera hastata
Psychophora sabini
Gynoephora groenlandica
Sulphur butterfly
Colias boothi
Pink-edged sulphur butterfly
Colias interior
Common sulphur
Colias hecla

Bog fritillary
Boloria eunomia
Polaris fritillary
Boloria polaris
Arctic fritillary
Boloria chariclea
Arctic blue
Pelbeius aquilo
American copper
Lycaena phloeas

BEETLES
Water beetle
Agabus moestus
Ground beetle
Amara alpina
Fungus beetle
Lathridius minimus
Tortoise beetle
Metriochemus obscuripes

WASPS, SAWFLIES and BEES
Bumble bee
Bombus polaris
Bombus hyperboreus
Ichneumon wasps
Mesoleius sp.
Ichneumon lariae
Ichneumon amauroplis
Ichneumon erythomelas
Ichneuman erythomelas

TWO-WINGED FLIES
Crane fly
Tipula arctica
Nephrotoma arcticola
Chironomidae
Sandfly
Ceratopogon sp.
Mosquito
Culicidae
Aedes impiger
Aedes nigripes
Hover fly
Syrphidae
Helophilus borealis
Sericomyia sexfasciatus
Metasyrphus chillcotti
Phalacrodira nigropilosa
Calliphoridae
Carrion fly
Borealius atriceps
Northern blowfly
Phormia terraenovae

Arctic midge
Chironomus polaris
Trichotanypus posticalis
Protanypus caudatus
Diamesa arctica
Cricotopus alpicola
Diplocladius bilobatus
Psectrocladius barbatimanus
Chaetocladius adsimilis
Lymnophyes borealis
Smittia polaris
Microspecta insignilobus

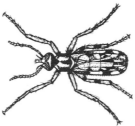

Blood-sucking midges
Ceratopogonidae
Forcipomyia sp.
Tachinid fly
Tachinidae
Spoggosia gelida
Peleteriopsis aenea
Dung fly
Muscidae
Scatophaga multisetosa
Scatophaga apicalis
Scatophaga nigripalpis
Cabbage maggot
Anthomyiinae
Hylemya fasciventris
Pegomyia arctica
Pegomyia tunicata
Muscoid fly
Limnophorinae
Spilgona almquisti
Spilgona deflorata
Spilgona dorsata
Spilgona obsoleta
Spilgona tundrae

BLACKFLIES
Gymnopais sp.
Prosimulium ursinum
Cnephia eremites
Cnephia borealis
Seal louse
Lepidophthirius macrohini

Louse
Hoplopleura acanthopus
SEA ANEMONES
Hacampa arctica
Bunodactis stella
Tapeworm
Echinococcus granulosus
Roundworm
Trichinella spiralis
Sea worm
Nemertina
Amphiporus angulatus
Marine worm
Priapulida
Priapulus caudata
Scale worm
Polychaeta
Harmothoe imbricata
Lug worm
Arenicola marina

MOLLUSCS
Clams
Pelecypods
Thin nut shell
Nucula tenuis
Sulcate nut shell
Nuculana tenuisulcata
Stout nut shell
Nuculana buccata
Mya-like yoldia
Yoldia myalis
Arctic yoldia
Yoldia arctica
Iceland scallop
Chlamys islandicus
Prickly jingle shell
Anomia aculeata
Blue mussel
Mytilus edulis
Horse mussel
Volsella modiolus

Smooth discord musculus
Musculus discors

Wrinkled musculus
Musculus corrugatus

Black musculus
Musculus niger

Faba crenella
Crenella faba

Glandular crenella
Crenella glandula

Fragile spoon shell
Periploma fragilis

Conrad's thracia
Thracia conradi

Large pandora
Pandora glacialis

Rostrate dipper
Cuspidaria rostrata

Black clam
Arctica islandica

Waved astarte
Astarte undata

Striate astarte
Astrate striata

Northern heart shell
Venericardia borealis

Iceland cockle
Clinocardium ciliatum

Northern dwarf cockle
Cerastoderma pinnulatum

Greenland cockle
Seripes groenlandicus

Venus shell
Liocyma fluctuosa

Little macoma
Macoma balthica

Chalky macoma
Macoma calcarea

Stimpson's surf clam
Spisula polynyma

Dwarf turton clam
Turtonia minuta

Long-neck clam
Mya arenaria

Short clam
Mya truncata

Arctic saxiclave
Hiatella arctica

Northern propeller clam
Cyrtodaria siliqua

Great piddock
Zirphaea crispata

Common shipworm
Teredo navalis

SNAILS

Tortoise shell limpet
Acmaea testudinalis

Little puncturella
Puncturella noachina

Cup-and-saucer
Cricibulum striatum

Northern rosy top shell
Margarites costalis

Smooth top shell
Margarites helicinus

Wavy top shell
Margarites groenlandica

Ladder shell
Epitorium groenlandicum

Waller's aclis
Aclis walleri

Iceland moon-shell
Amauropsis islandica

Greenland moon-shell
Lunatia groenlandica

Arctic natica
Natica clausa

Common velvet shell
Velutina laevigata

Cap shell
Capulus ungaricus

Orb shell
Skenea planorbis

Common periwinkle
Littorina littorea

Smooth periwinkle
Littorina obtusata

Northern rough periwinkle
Littorina saxatilis

Common Atlantic chink shell
Lacuna vincta

Pale chink shell
Lacuna pallidula

American pelican's foot
Aporrhais occidentalis

Atlantic dogwinkle
Thais lapillis

Trophon
Trophon clathratus
Trophon scalariformes

Rock purple
Thais lapillus

Common northern whelk
Buccinum undatum

Stimpson's spindle shell
Colus stimpsoni

Common northern neptune
Neptunea despecta

Kroyer's plicifusus
Plicifusus kroyeri

Noble bela
Lora nobilis

Common northern admete
Admete couthouyi

Needle shell
Turritellopsis acicula

Brown's barrel-bubble
Cylichna alba

Arctic barrel-bubble
Retusa obtusa

CRUSTACEANS

Common rock barnacle
Balanus balanoides

Northern ridged barnacle
Balanus balanus

Notched acorn barnacle
Balanus crenatus

ECHINODERMS

Polar starfish
Leptasterias polaris

Blood sea-star
Henrica sanguinolenta

Green sea urchin
Strongylocentrotus droebachiensis

Sea squirt
Tunicata
Ascidia callosa

FISHES

LAMPREYS

Lake sturgeon
Entosphenus japonicus

STURGEONS

Lake sturgeon
Acipenser fulvescens

Atlantic sturgeon
Acipenser oxyrhynchus

HERRINGS

Pacific herring
Clupea harengus

SALMONS and TROUTS

Brook (char) trout
Salvelinus fontinalis

Arctic char
Salvelinus alpinus

Lake trout
Salvelinus namaycush

Atlantic salmon
Salmo salar

Lake whitefish
Coregonus clupeaformis

Broad whitefish
Coregonus nasus

Round whitefish
Prosopium cylindraceum

Cisco (lake herring)
Coregonus artedii

Inconnu
Stenodus leucichthys

Smelts
Osmeridae

Capelin
Mallotus villosus

SHARKS

Greenland shark
Somniosus microcephalus

Atlantic prickly skate
Raja radiata

Spiny dogfish
Squalus acanthias

PIKES

Northern pike
Exos lucius

SUCKERS

Longnose sucker
Catostomus catostomus

Northern redhorse
Moxostoma macrolepidotum

MINNOWS

Emerald shiner
Notropis atherinoides

Spottail shiner
Notropis hudsonius

LANTERN FISH

Glacial lanternfish
Benthosema glaciale

CODS

Burdot
Lota lota

Arctic cod
Boreogadus saida

Saffron cod
Elginus navaga

Atlantic cod
Gadus morhua

Pacific tomcod
Microgadus proximus

Greenland cod
Gadus ogac

Rough-head grenadier
Macrourus berglax

STICKLEBACKS

Threespine stickleback
Gasterosteus aculeatus

Ninespine stickleback
Pungitius pungitius

Brook stickleback
Eucalia inconstans

WOLF FISH

Anarhichas denticulatus

SNAKEBLENNY

Fourline snakeblenny
Eumesogrammus praecisus

Spotted snakeblenny
Stichaeus punctatus

Stout eelblenny
Lumpenus medius

Slender eelblenny
Lumpenus fabricii

EELPOUT

Pale eelpout
Lycodes pallidus

Arctic eelpout
Lycodes reticulatus

Polar eelpout
Lycodes turneri

SANDLANCE

Arctic sandlance
Ammodytes hexapterus

Dubius sandlance
Ammodytes dubius

ROSEFISH

Sebastes marinus

SCULPINS

Hookeye sculpin
Artediellus uncinatus

Arctic staghorn sculpin
Gymnocanthus tricuspis

Twohorn sculpin
Icelus bicornis

Fourhorn sculpin
Myoxocephalus quadricornis

Arctic sculpin
Myoxocephalus scorpioides

Shorthorn sculpin
Myoxocephalus scorpius

Slimy sculpin
Cottus cognatus

Mailed sculpin
Triglops nybelini

Ribbed sculpin
Triglops pingelii

SEAPOACHER

Alligator fish
Aspidophoroides monopterygius

Arctic seapoacher
Aspidophoroides olrikii

Sturgeon-like seapoacher
Agonus acipenseringus

LUMPSUCKER

Lumpfish
Cyclopterus lumpus

Leatherfin lumpsucker
Eumicrotremus derjugini

Spiny lumpsucker
Eumicrotremus spinosus

Gelatinous seasnail
Liparis koefoedi

RIGHTEYE FLOUNDERS

Greenland halibut
Reinhardtius hippoglossoides

Arctic flounder
Liopsetta glacialis

Smooth flounder
Liopsetta putnami

Starry flounder
Platichthys stellatus

BIRDS
Found in Summer only

Common loon
Gavia immer

Yellow-billed loon
Gavia adamsii

Arctic loon
Gavia arctica

Red-throated loon
Gavia stellata

Fulmar
Fulmarus glacialis

Whistling swan
Olor columbianus

Canada goose
Branta canadensis

Brant goose
Branta bernicla

Black brant
Branta nigricans

White-fronted goose
Anser albifrons

Snow goose
Chen hyperborea

Blue goose
Chen caerulescens

Ross's goose
Anser rossii

Pintail
Anas acuta

Oldsquaw
Clangula hyemalis

Common eider
Somateria mollissima

King eider
Somateria spectabilis

White winged scoter
Melanitta deglandi

Red-breasted merganser
Mergus serrator

Rough-legged hawk
Buteo lagopus

Golden eagle
Aquila chrysaetos

Peregrine falcon
Falco peregrinus

Sandhill crane
Grus canadensis

Ringed plover
Charadrius hiaticula

Semipalmated plover
Charadrius semipalmatus

Golden plover
Pluvialis dominica

Blackbellied plover
Squatarola squatarola

Ruddy turnstone
Arenaria interpres

Whimbrel
Numenius phaeous

Eskimo curlew (possibly extinct)
Numenius borealis

Harlequin duck
Histrionicus histrionicus

Knot
Calidris canutus
Purple sandpiper
Erolia maritima
Pectoral sandpiper
Erolia melanotos
White-rumped sandpiper
Erolia fuscicollis
Baird's sandpiper
Erolia bairdii
Dunlin
Erolia alpina
Stilt sandpiper
Micropalama himantopus
Semipalmated sandpiper
Ereunetes pusillus
Buff-breasted sandpiper
Tryngites subruficollis
Hudsonian godwit
Limosa haemastica

Sanderling
Crocethia alba
Red phalarope
Phalaropus fulicarius
Northern phalarope
Lobipes lobatus
Pomarine jaeger
Stercorarius pomarinus
Parasitic jaeger
Stercorarius parasiticus
Long-tailed jaeger
Stercorarius longicaudus
Glaucous gull
Larus hyperboreus
Iceland gull
Larus glaucoides
Great black-backed gull
Larus Marinis
Herring gull
Larus argentatus
Thayer's gull
Larus thayeri

Ivory gull
Pagophila eburnea
Black-legged kittiwake
Rissa tridactyla
Ross's gull
Rhodostethia rosea
Sabine's gull
Xema sabini
Arctic tern
Sterna paradisaea
Short-eared owl
Asio flammeus
Horned lark
Eromophila alpestris
Wheatear
Oenanthe oenanthe
Water pipit
Anthus spinoletta
Hoary redpoll
Acanthis hornemanni
Common redpoll
Acanthis flammea
Savannah sparrow
Passerculus sandwichensis
Tree sparrow
Spizella arborea
White-crowned sparrow
Zonotrichia leucophrys
Lapland longspur
Calcarius lapponicus
Snow bunting
Plectrophenax nivalis

BIRDS

Found all year around

Gyrfalcon
Falco rusticolus
Willow ptarmigan
Lagopus lagopus
Rock ptarmigan
Lagopus mutus
Thick-billed murre
Uria lomvia
Dovekie
Plautus alle
Black guillemot
Cepphus grylle
Snowy owl
Nyctea scandiaca
Common raven
Corvus corax

LAND MAMMALS

SHREWS
Masked shrew
Sorex cinereus
Arctic shrew
Sorex arcticus

HARES
Arctic hare
Lepus arcticus

SQUIRRELS
Arctic ground squirrel
Citellus parryi

BEARS
Barren ground grizzly
Ursus arctos

Polar bear
Thalarctos maritimus

MICE
Red-backed vole
Clethrionomys rutilus
Tundra vole
Microtus oecoromus
Collared lemming
Discrostonyx groenlandicus
Brown lemming
Lemmus trimucronatus

WOLVES and FOXES
Arctic fox
Alopex lagopus
Arctic wolf
Canis lupus

WEASLES, FERRETS and MINKS
Ermine
Mustela erminea
Least weasel
Mustela rixosa
Wolverine
Gulo gulo

DEER
Barren-ground caribou
Rangifer arcticus

Peary's caribou
Rangifer tarandus

CATTLE
Musk ox
Ovibos moschatus

SEA MAMMALS

WHALES, DOLPHINS and PORPOISES
Right and bowhead whales
Balaenidae
Greenland bowhead whale
Balaena mysticetus
Finback whales
Balaenopteridae
Common finback
Balaenoptera physalus
Lesser rorqual
Balaenoptera acutorostrata
Blue whale
Sibbaldus musculus
Humpback whale
Megaptera novaeangliae
Killer whale
Orcinus orca
Harbour porpoise
Phocoena phocoena
White whale
Delphinapterus leucas
Narwhal
Monodon monoceros

SEA LIONS and SEALS
Ringed seal
Phoca hispida
Harbour seal
Pusa vitulina
Hooded seal
Cystophora cristata
Bearded seal
Erignathus barbatus
Atlantic walrus
Odobenus rosmarus

Harp seal
Pagophilus groenlandica

REGIONAL MAPS AND INFORMATION

Large-scale maps and other information on the Arctic coast region can be obtained at moderate cost from: Government of Canada, Department of Energy, Mines, and Resources, 601 Booth Street, Ottawa, Ontario; Information Service, Government of the North West Territories, Yellowknife, N.W.T.; Department of Indian Affairs and Northern Development, Ottawa, Ontario. A selection of film strips and slides is available from: National Film Board, P.O. Box 6100, Montreal 3, P.Q.

BIBLIOGRAPHY

REGIONAL

BAIRD, P. D.
The Polar World.
New York: Wiley and Sons, 1964.

BIRKET-SMITH, KAJ.
The Eskimos.
London: Methuen & Co., 1959.

DUNBAR, M. and GREENAWAY, K. R.
Arctic Canada from the Air.
Ottawa: Queen's Printer, 1956.

FREUCHEN, PETER.
Book of the Eskimos.
New York: World Publishing, 1961.

HEARNE, SAMUEL. (J. B. Tyrell, ed.)
A Journey from Prince of Wales's Fort to the Northern Arctic Ocean.
Toronto: Champlain Society, 1911.

KIMBLE, G. H. T. and GOOD, D. (eds.)
Geography of the Northlands.
New York: Wiley and Sons, 1955.

MACDONALD, R. ST. J. (ed.)
The Arctic Frontier.
University of Toronto Press, 1966.

MIRSKY, J.
To the Arctic.
New York: Alfred A. Knopf, 1948.

NANSEN, FRIDTJOF.
In Northern Mists.
London: W. Heinemann, 1911.

PIKE, W.
The Barren Ground of Northern Canada.
London: Macmillan, 1892.

PIRIE, A.
Fallout.
London: MacGibbon & Kee, 1958.

SETON, E. T.
The Arctic Prairies.
New York: Scribner's, 1912.

SMITH, I. N. (ed.)
The Unbelievable Land.
Ottawa: Queen's Printer, 1964.

STEFANSSON, VILHJALMUR.
The Friendly Arctic.
London: Macmillan, 1943.

WILKINSON, DOUG.
Land of the Long Day.
Toronto: Clarke, Irwin, 1955.

WILSON, J. TUZO
The Year of the New Moons.
New York: Knopf, 1961.

CLIMATE

GEIGER, R.
The Climate near the Ground.
Cambridge: Harvard University Press, 1950.

RAE, R. W.
Climate of the Canadian Arctic Archipelago.
Ottawa: Queen's Printer, 1951.

SUTTON, O. G.
Understanding the Weather.
London: Penguin Books, 1960.

THOMAS, M. K.
Canadian Arctic Temperatures.
Ottawa: Dept. of Transport, Meteorological Branch, Circular 3334, 1960.

THOMPSON, H. A.
The Climate of the Canadian Arctic.
Ottawa: Queen's Printer, 1967.

WILSON, H. P., MARKHAM, W. E., DEWAR, S. W., and THOMPSON, H. A.
Weather in the Canadian Arctic.
Ottawa: Dept. of Transport, Meteorological Branch, Circular 2387.

PERIODICAL

HARE, F. K. and MONTGOMERY, M. R.
"Ice, Open Water and Winter Climate in the Eastern Arctic of North America."
Arctic (Montreal), Volume 2, 1949.

GEOLOGY

BLACKADAR, R. G.
Geological Reconnaissance North Coast of Ellesmere Island.
Ottawa: Geological Survey of Canada, Paper 53-10, 1954.

CHAPMAN, SYDNEY.
The Earth's Magnetism.
London: Methuen & Co., 1951.

CRAIG, B. G. and FYLES, J. G.
Pleistocene Geology of Arctic Canada.
Ottawa: Geological Survey of Canada, Paper 60-10, 1960.

DUNBAR, C. O.
The Earth.
London: Weidenfeld & Nicholson, 1966.

DUNBAR, C. O.
Historical Geology. (2nd ed.)
New York: Wiley and Sons, 1960.

FLINT, R. F.
Glacial and Pleistocene Geology.
New York: Wiley and Sons, 1957.

FORTIER, Y. O., MCNAIR, A. H.
and THORSTEINSSON, R.
*Geology and Petroleum Possibilities
in Canadian Arctic Islands.*
Bulletin American Ass'n. Petroleum
Geology, Volume 38, No. 10, 1954.

JEFFREYS, H.
The Earth.
Cambridge University Press, 1959.

LANG, A. H.,
Prospecting in Canada.
Ottawa: Queen's Printer, 1960.

MOORE, E. S.
Elementary Geology for Canada.
Toronto: J. M. Dent & Sons, 1944.

SABENA, A. P.
Rock and Mineral Collecting in Canada.
Ottawa: Queen's Printer, Vol. 1,
Yukon, Northwest Territories and
British Columbia, 1965.

STOCKWELL, C. H.
Geology and Economic Minerals of Canada.
Ottawa: Queen's Printer, 1957.

STONMEN, C.
The Polar Aurora.
Oxford, Clarendon Press, 1955.

THORSTEINSSON, R. and TOZER, E. T.
*Summary Account of Structural History of
the Canadian Arctic Archipelago since
Precambrian Times.*
Ottawa: Geological Survey of Canada,
Paper 60-7, 1960.

TYRELL, J. W.
*Across the Sub-Arctic of Canada, A Journey
of 3,000 Miles by Canoe and Snowshoe
through the Barren Lands.*
London: T. Fisher Unwin, 1898.

ICE

KING, T.
Water, Miracle of Nature.
New York: Macmillan, 1953.

MACKAY, J. R.
The Mackenzie Delta Area, N.W.T.
Ottawa: Queen's Printer, 1963.

MULLER, FRITZ.
*Preliminary Report 1961-62 of the
Axel Heiberg Island Research Project.*
Montreal: McGill University Press, 1963.

NANSEN, F.
Farthest North.
New York: Harper Bros., 1897.

PAPANIN, I. D.
Life on an Ice Floe
New York: Messner, 1939.

PEARY, R. E.
The North Pole.
London: Hodder & Stoughton, 1910.

WRIGHT, G. F.
The Ice Age in North America.
New York: Appleton & Co., 1889.

PERIODICALS

BILELLO, M. A.
"Formation, Growth and Decay of Sea Ice
in the Canadian Arctic Archipelago."
Arctic (Montreal), Vol. 14, No. 1, 1961.

FLINT, R. F.
"The Ice Age in the North American Arctic."
Arctic (Montreal), Vol. 5, No. 3, 1952.

KOENIG, L. S., GREENAWAY, K. R.,
DUNBAR, M., and HATTERSLY-SMITH, G.
"Arctic Ice Islands."
Arctic (Montreal), Vol. 5, No. 2, 1952.

RAY, L. L.
"Permafrost."
Arctic (Montreal), Vol. 4, No. 3, 1951.

SHARP, R. P.
"Glaciers in the Arctic."
Arctic (Montreal), Vol. 9, Nos. 1
and 2, 1956.

TEDROW, J. C. F. and CANTLON, J. E.
"Concepts of Soil Formation and
Classification in Arctic Regions."
Arctic (Montreal), Vol. 11, No. 3, 1958.

PLANTS

BESCHEL, R. E.
*Botany, and Some Remarks on the History
of Vegetation and Glacierization.*
Montreal: McGill University Press, 1961.

Flora, Fauna and Geology.
Ottawa: Dept. of Northern Affairs
and National Resources, 1954.

POLUNIN, NICHOLAS.
Circumpolar Arctic Flora.
Oxford University Press, 1959.

POLUNIN, NICHOLAS.
*Botany of the Canadian Eastern
Arctic.* Parts 1 and 2.
Ottawa: Queen's Printer, 1947-48.

PORSILD, A. E.
*Illustrated Flora of the Canadian
Arctic Archipelago.*
Ottawa: Queen's Printer, 1964.

SAVILLE, D. B. O.
*Botany of the Northwestern
Queen Elizabeth Islands.*
Ottawa: Dept. Mines & Tech. Surveys,
Geography Branch, Memoir 3, 1961.

PERIODICAL

BLISS, L. C.
"Adaptations of Arctic and Alpine
Plants to Environmental Conditions."
Arctic (Montreal), Vol. 15, No. 2, 1962.

ANIMALS

ANDERSON, R. M.
Catalogue of Canadian Recent Mammals.
Ottawa: National Museum of Canada,
Bulletin 102.

BANFIELD, A. W. F.
*Preliminary Investigation of
the Barren Ground Caribou.*
Ottawa: Queen's Printer, 1954.

CLARKE, C. H. D.
*A Biological Investigation of the
Thelon Game Sanctuary.*
Ottawa: National Museum of Canada, 1940.

DUNBAR, M. J.
Eastern Arctic Waters.
Ottawa: Fisheries Res. Board,
Bulletin 88, 1951.

GODFREY, W. E.
The Birds of Canada.
Ottawa: Queen's Printer, 1966.

HARINGTON, C. R.
Denning Habits of the Polar Bear.
Ottawa: Canadian Wildlife Service,
Paper No. 5, 1968.

KELSALL, J. P.
*Barren Ground Caribou Movements
in the Canadian Arctic.*
Washington: Wildlife Management
Institute, 1955.

KELSALL, J. P.
*The Migratory Barren Ground
Caribou of Canada.*
Ottawa: Queen's Printer, 1968.

MANSFIELD, A. W.
Seals of Arctic and Eastern Canada.
Ottawa: Queen's Printer, 1964.

PEDERSON, A.
Polar Animals.
London: Harrap & Co., 1962.

SETON, E. T.
The Arctic Prairies.
Toronto: Wm. Briggs, 1911.

SCHOLANDER, P. F., HOCK, R.,
WALTERS, U., and IRVING, L.
*Adaptations to Cold in Arctic and Tropical
Mammals and Birds in Relation to Body
Temperature, Insulation and Basal
Metabolic Rate.*
Ottawa: Biological Bulletin, 99: 259-271.

SNYDER, L. L.
Arctic Birds of Canada.
University of Toronto Press, 1957.

SYMINGTON, F.
Tuktu.
Ottawa: Queen's Printer, 1965.

TENER, J. S.
Muskoxen in Canada.
Ottawa: Queen's Printer, 1965.

PERIODICALS

BUTLER, L.
"The Nature of Cycles in Populations
of Canadian Mammals."
Canadian Zoology (Toronto), Vol. 313, 1953.

FAY, F. H.
"Carnivorous Walrus and Some
Arctic Zoonoses."
Arctic (Montreal), Vol. 13, No. 2, 1960.

HOHN, E. O.
"Lemmings, Hares and Hormones."
The Beaver (Winnipeg), Winter, 1961.

HOHN, E. O.
"Birds in the Arctic."
The Beaver (Winnipeg), Summer, 1959.

IRVING, L. and KROG, J.
"Body Temperature of Arctic and
Sub-Arctic Birds and Mammals."
Journal of App. Phys., Volume 6, 1954.

LOUGHERY, ALAN G.
"The Polar Bear and its Protection."
Oryx (Washington), Vol. 3, No. 5, 1956.

PRUITT, W. O.
"A New Caribou Problem."
The Beaver (Winnipeg), Winter, 1962.

PRUITT, W. O.
"Snow as a Factor in the Winter
Ecology of the Barren Ground Caribou."
Arctic (Montreal), Vol. 12, No. 3, 1954.

RAND, A. L.
"The Ice Age and Mammal
Speciation in North America."
Arctic (Montreal), Vol. 7, No. 1, 1954.

TWINN, C. R.
"Studies of the Biology and Control
of Biting Flies in Northern Canada."
Arctic (Montreal), Vol. 3, 1950.

INDEX

A

Active layer of permafrost, 56
Admiralty Inlet, 22
Adrenal gland, 127, 128, 129
Africa, 132
Airstrips, and snow, 20
Alaska, 49, 128, 141
Algae, 70
  marine, 70
Alpine glaciers, 30
Amphipods, 112
Amundsen Gulf, 139
Antarctic, 101, 106
Antlers, caribou, 129
Appalachians, 44
Arctic char, 111, 112, 133
Arctic cod, 112
Arctic cotton grass, 8, 18, 70
Arctic fox, 102, 104, 126,
  127, 133, 140
Arctic grayling, 112
Arctic ground squirrel, 55, 104
  hibernation, 104
Arctic halibut, 111
Arctic hare, 124, 126, 133
Arctic heather, 69
Arctic lupine, 68
Arctic Ocean, 49
Arctic poppy, 18
Arctic sorrel grass, 70
Arteries, 104
Arthropods, 101
Asexual reproduction, 78
Asia, 132, 135
Atlantic cod, 111
Atlantic Ocean, 49, 135
Atomic bomb, 142
Auk family, 94
Aurora borealis, 23
Axel Heiberg Island, 18, 30, 43

B

Bacteria, in soil, 53
Baffin Bay, 49
Baffin Island, 18, 22, 26, 29, 43,
  44, 49, 70, 92, 95, 96, 112,
  124, 135, 136, 139

Baker Lake, 28, 78
Baleen, 136
Baleen whale, 114
Banks Island, 44
Barren ground caribou, 129,
  see caribou
Barren ground grizzly, 92, 104
Basaltic rock, 42
Bay ice, 26
Bearded seal, 114, 116, 117
Beaufort Sea, 27, 139
Bees, 101
Beluga, 115
Bergs, 30
Bergschrund, 29
Bering Strait, 49
Berries, 70, 95
Between-Glacier Lake, 30
Biome, 52, 76, 95, 103, 126, 133
Birch, creeping, 69, 78, 126
Birds, 92, 125
  adaptation to cold, 93-94
  distraction techniques, 96
  food, 95
  nesting, 96
Blackbird, 106
Blizzard, 19, 20, 49
Blowfly, 126
  larvae, 101
Blubber, 136, 137
Body heat,
  birds, 94
  mammals, 103
Bog, 28, 56, 68
Brash ice, 26
Breathing hole, seal, 118, 133
Brine fly, 101
British Columbia, 49
Brood nest, 96
Butterfly, 101
Bylot Island, 95, 96

C

Cake ice, 26
Calves, musk ox, 105
Canadian shield, 42-44, 111, 142
  mountain-building, 42
  trough of, 43
Candled ice, 28
Cape Bathurst, 140

Caribou, 53, 55, 92, 101, 124,
  126, 132, 133, 134, 135,
  140, 141
  food of, 142
  life cycle, 126-131
  migration, 106, 129
Caribou moss, 69, 141
Cape Columbia, 52
Carnivores, 116, 131
Cathay, 135
Cenozoic era, 47
Centipede, 126
Cesium-137, 142
Cetaceans, 115
Chantry Inlet, 135
Char, Arctic, 111, 112
Chukchee Sea, 139
Churchill, 55
Cladonia, 70
Clams, 116
Climate, 44, 52, 95, 111
  during glacial age, 47
Clothing, 132
Cloud cover, 76
Cluster moss, 76
Cod, 111, 112
Cod, polar, 118
Colonizing plants, 78
Colour cycle of plants, 69-70
Committee Bay, 96
Conservation, 134
Continental shelf, 111
Copepods, 112, 118
Copper, 142
Coppermine River, 112
Cordillera, 44
  during glacial age, 47, 49
Corona, 23
Coronation Gulf, 111
Cotton grass, 52, 70
Courtship, birds, 96
Cretaceous, 44
Crevasses, 29
Cross-pollination, 78
Crowberry, 126
Crust, formation of, 42
Crustaceans, 118
Curlew, 95
Cushion plants, 76, 78
Cuticle, 70
Cycles, 127-129, 134, 135
Cyclonic wind, 22
Cysts, 126

D

Davis Strait, 138
Day length, 23
Deciduous forests, 69
Deer, 129
Delayed implantation, 114
Diatom, 117-118
Digges Island, 96
Dismal Lakes, 52
Displacement activity, 106
Distant Early Warning Line, 55
Diurnal cycles, 76
Dog, Husky, 92-93, 103,
  124, 133
Dormancy, 101, 104
Dovekie, 93
Drift patterns, 19
Drumlin hills, 50

E

Earthworm, 101
Echinococcus granulosis, 126
Eclipse Sound, 116, 124
Ecology, of tundra, 52
Edible plants, 70
Edmonton, 55
Ellesmere Island, 18, 29, 43,
  44, 52, 55, 69, 70, 96
England, 136
Erosion, 42, 53
Erratic boulders, 50
Eskers, 18, 50
Eskimo, 53, 103, 104, 111,
  112, 114, 116, 124, 134,
  135, 141, 142
Eskimo Lakes, 115
Experimental farm, 68

F

Farms, 18
Feathers, 93, 94
Fiord, 22
Fish, 28, 111, 135
  primitive, 111
Fleas, 126
Flies, 126
Floe ice, 27
Flowers, 76, 78,
Fog, 22

Food chain, 68, 123, 124, 131, 135, 142
Fort Prince of Wales, 101
Fossils, 50, 111
Fox, 96, 102, 104, 126, 127, 133, 140
Foxe Basin, 19, 27
Free-floating ice, 26
Freshwater fish, 111
Freshwater ice, 28
Frobisher Bay, 26, 112, 116
Frobisher, Martin, 136
Frost, 18, 53, 55
  action, 56
  effect on plants, 55
Fullerton, 139
Fulmar, 96
Fungus, 70
Fur, 102, 105, 106, 112, 129, 140

G

Gabriel, The, 136
Gas, 142
Geese, 95, 133
Genetic diversity, 78
Glacial age, 47
Glacial debris, 29
Glacial ice, 18, 21, 22, 29, 30, 44, 47, 49, 50, 55
  and plant colonization, 78
  erosion by, 50
  fluctuation of, 49
  forming of, 47
  melting of, 49
Glacial lake, 30, 50
Glacial soils, 53
Glacial till, 30, 50
Glacier, 29, 30, 132
  forming of, 47
  gouging of, 50
  melting of, 49
  Thompson, 30, 78
  White, 30, 78
Glare, 104
Gold, 136
Grain weevil, 101
Granite, 42
Grasses, 69, 125
  cotton, 70
  sorrel, 70

Graylings, 111, 112
Great Bear Lake, 52
Greenland, 135, 138
Greenland right whale, 111, 136
Greenland Sea, 49, 138
Greenland shark, 112
Grizzly, barren ground, 92, 104
Ground-drift, 20-22
Ground squirrel, 55, 104, 126, 131
Grouse, 94
Growlers, 26
Growth rings, 78
Guard hair, musk ox, 106
Guillemot, black, 93, 95
Gulf of Mexico, 49
Gull, 95
Gyrfalcon, 93, 126

H

Halibut, Arctic, 111
Hares, 102, 104, 124, 126, 133
Harpoon, 132, 135
Harp seal, 116
Hawk, 95
Heat, and ice, 28
Heat loss, mammals, 101
Heat regulation, 103-104
Herbivores, 104, 126, 133
Herschel Island, 139, 140
Hibernation, 69, 70, 92, 101, 104
  Arctic ground squirrel, 104
Honeycombed ice, 26
Hooded seal, 117
Hudson Bay, 18, 27, 42, 43, 50, 53, 55, 106, 111, 138
  during glacier, 47, 49
  forming of, 50
  uplift of, 50
Hudson Bay Railway, 56
Hummock, 18, 26

I

Iceberg, 19, 26, 27, 30
Ice-blink, 26
Ice caps, 47, 49
Ice, definitions of, 26
  freshwater, 28
  land-fast, 27
  pack ice, 27

Ice-foot, 26, 27
Ice tongue, 26
Idlouk, 124
Igloo, 132
Infectious diseases, 129
Insectivore, 126
Insects, 95, 101, 104, 125, 126
Insulation in mammals, 103
Iron, 142
Iron pyrite, 136
Ivory, 132, 139, 140

J

Jackfish, 111
Jaeger, 95, 96, 126, 128
James Bay, 50, 94
Jar, 117
Jones Sound, 112
Juniper, 78

K

Kadloonak Island, 136
Kayak, 26, 132
Kazan Falls, 28
Kazan River, 28
Killer whale, 114-115, 116, 118
King William Island, 19
Kittiwakes, 96

L

Labrador, 44, 49
Lactation, musk ox, 106
Lakes,
  and fish, 111
  and ice, 28
  postglacial, 53
Lake Hazen, 55
Lake trout, 112
Land bridge, 49
Land-fast ice, 26, 117, 136
Lark, 94
Larvae, warble fly, 126
Lava, 42
Lemmings, Arctic, 68, 104, 126, 131
  cycles, 128
Lice, 126
Lichen, 18, 22, 50, 55, 69, 78, 125, 126, 128

and radioactive fallout, 141
  life cycle, 70
Limpets, 112
Liver of musk ox, 104
Longspur, 95
Loon, 95, 96
Lowland, 18
Lupines, Arctic, 68

M

Mackenzie Delta, 111
Mackenzie River, 55
Magma, 42
Mammals, 68, 69, 93, 94, 101, 134
  hibernation, 104
Mammoth, 92
Marco Polo, 135
Marine beaches, 18, 50
McGill Ice Cap, 30
Meighen Island, 101
Melting of ice, 28
Melville Bay, 138
Mesozoic era, 47
Metabolism, 101
  in birds, 94
  in mammals, 103
  in plants, 76
Meta Incognita, 136
Metamorphic rock, 42
Mice, 104, 126
Micro-environment of plants, 70
Migration, 95, 106, 128, 129
  of caribou, 129-130
Migratory birds, 52
Midges, 126
Misto, 118
Mites, 126
Moraine, 29, 30
Mosquito, 101, 126
Moss, 18, 125, 126, 129, 131
Moulting, 96
Mountain-building, 42, 44
Murre, thick-billed, 93
Mushrooms, 70
Musk ox, 52, 53, 55, 92, 102, 126, 131, 140, 141
  adaptation to Arctic, 104
  defensive mechanisms, 106
  nutrition, 105
  reproductive cycle, 105-106

Mutation, 96
Mysis, 118

N

Narwhal, 111, 115-116
National Museum, 68
Nectar, 125
Nelson River, 56
Nesting, 96
Niche, 52
Nickel, 142
Nitrogen, in soil, 18, 53,
  in plants, 55
  in protein synthesis, 105
Northern development, 142
Northern Lights, 23
Northern pike, 111
Northwest Passage, 136
Norwegian Sea, 138
Nuliakjuk, 134

O

Ocean, and glaciers, 47
Oil, 142
Oil lamp, 132
Ostracoderms, 111
Ostrapods, 112
Overcrowding, 128
Overgrazing, 131
Over-wintering in plants, 78
Owl, snowy, 93, 126

P

Pacific Ocean, 111
Pack ice, 26, 118
  breakup of, 27
Pancake ice, 26
Palaeozoic, 44
Parasites, 126
Peary caribou, 129
Pelage of caribou, 103
Pelly Bay, 50, 96, 135
Perennials, 70
Permafrost, 55-56
  effect on drainage, 56
  formation of, 55

Petroleum flies, 101
Phalarope, 95, 96
Photosynthesis, 76, 117, 125
Physiography, 43
Pike, 111, 112
Pituitary gland, 104, 128
Plains, 18, 47
Plankton, 118
Plant Research Institute, 68
Plants, 68
  adaptations, 69, 70, 78
  and snow, 76
  colour cycle, 69
  edible, 70
  effect of permafrost, 56
  freezing of seeds, 68
  frost action, 55
  growth, 70, 78
  nitrogen in, 53-54
  seashore community, 69
  seed production, 78
Plateaux, 18, 29, 43, 47
Pleistocene, 44, 47, 49, 55, 132
Poisonous plants, 70
Polar bear, 92, 102, 104, 106,
  111, 118, 133, 134, 139,
  140, 141
Polar sea, 49, 50
Polar zone, 106
Pollination, 78
Polyanas, 26
Polygon formations, 56
Polymerized water
  molecules, 118
Ponds, 26
Poppy, Arctic, 69, 78
Population cycles, 128
Porsild, A. E., 68
Precambrian, 43, 44
Precambrian rocks, 43
Predator, 116, 126, 133
Pressure, 47
Pressure ridges, 26
Proto-earth, 42
Prince of Wales Island, 44
Ptarmigan, 93, 94, 96, 126
Puff-balls, 70

R

Rabbit, 124
Radiation, 70

Radioactive fallout, 141
Rainfall, 8, 53
Raven, 92,
  and dogs, 93
Refugia, 132
Reindeer, 142
Reindeer moss, 70
Reproduction cycles, 104
Repulse Bay, 27
Rhubarb, 70
Right whale, 111, 136
Rime ice, 78
Rind ice, 26
Ringed seal, 114, 116, 117, 118
  breathing hole, 118
  young, 118
River ice, 28
Rock flour, 29, 53
Rock ptarmigan, 93-94
Rodents, 128
Roots, effect of frost, 55
  and permafrost, 56
  carbohydrate reserves, 76
  edible, 70
Rumen, 105
Russia, 142
Rutting, 131

S

Sahara Desert, 8
Sandhill crane, 94
Sandpiper, 94
Sand ridges, 50
Sandwort, 69
Saxifrage, 70, 126
Scandinavia, 128, 142
Scales of fish, 111
Scarcity and plenty, cycle, 135
Sculpin, 112, 116
Sea birds, 96
Sea canaries, 115
Sea, freezing of, 26
Sea ice, 26
Seal, 111, 112, 114, 124,
  132, 133, 135
  birth cycle, 114
Sealskin, 132, 133
Sea pink, 69
Seashore plants, 69
Seasons, 8, 23, 53
Seaweed, 70

Sedimentary rocks, 44, 47, 50
Seeds, 68, 70, 78, 104
  hibernation, 69
Self-pollination, 78
Sex glands, 128
Shale, 18
Shark, Greenland, 112
Shield, 42, 47
Shrews, 104, 126
Silver jar, 118
Simpson, Thomas, 52
Sinew, 133
Sled, 132, 133
Slush ice, 26
Snow, 8, 19-22
  and glaciers, 47, 49
  and musk ox, 106
  and plants, 76
  and wind, 21
  blizzards, 49
  compaction, 20
  drift pattern, 19
  ground-drift, 20
  white-out, 21-22
Snow-blindness, 22
Snow bunting, 93
Snow caves, 103
Snowfields, 29
Snow geese, 95, 96
Snowy owl, 93, 96
  and lemmings, 128
Soapstone, 132
Soil, 52, 68
  erosion and, 53
  fertility of, 53
  permafrost, 55
Soil creep, 56
Soilfluction, 56
Somerset Island, 44
Sorrel grass, Arctic, 70
Sparrow, 94
Spermaceti, 136, 137
Sperm whale, 136
Spider, 126
Square flipper, 117
Squirrel, ground, 55, 104
Steam-fog, 28
Stefansson, 101
Stickleback, 112
Strontium-90, 142
Suspended animation, 68
Swamps, 28, 56, 68
Symbiosis, 56, 96

T

Taboos, 134
Tapeworm, 126
Tay Sound, 124
Temperate zone, 95
Temperature, 8, 52, 69
  and freezing of lakes, 28
  and permafrost, 55
  and plants, 55, 76
  during glaciation, 49
  during Mesozoic era, 47
  of animals, 101
  of birds, 94
  of plants, 76
Terminus, 29
Tern, 126
Tertiary period, 44
Tetraonidae, 94
Thick-billed murre, 93
Thompson glacier, 30, 78
Thule Eskimo culture, 141

Tidal flats, plants, 69
Tide, 18, 19, 26, 112
Timber wolf, 131
Tom cod, 111
Tree line, 52, 131
Trout, lake, 112
Tundra wolf, 131
Turnstone, 94
Tusks, narwhal, 115-116
  walrus, 116

U

Umiak, 132
Ungava, 43
Uplift of land, 50

V

Vegetation, 69, 104
  in food cycle, 126

Vegetative reproduction, 76
Veins, 104
Victoria Island, 50
Vitamin A, 112
Volcano, 42

W

Walrus, 112, 116, 132, 133, 139
Warble fly, 126, 133
Water-sky, 26
Weapons, 133, 134
Weasel, 126
Whale, 114, 132, 133, 136,
  139, 140
Whalers, 135-141
Whaling, 136-139
Whelping period, 131
Whitefish, 111
White glacier, 30, 78

White-out, 21
White whale, 114, 115
Willow, dwarf, 69, 78, 104, 126
Willow ptarmigan, 93-94
Wind, 21, 22-23, 26, 27,
  54, 78, 112
  and pollination, 78
Wind-chill, 78
Winds, polar, 49
  during glaciation, 49
  effect on plants, 76
Wolves, 92, 103, 104, 106, 126,
  128, 129, 131, 133, 140
World Meteorological
  Organization, 26

Y

Young ice, 26
Yukon District, 8, 43, 47, 49

ACKNOWLEDGEMENTS

The author wishes to acknowledge with gratitude the advice and assistance given unstintingly throughout twenty years of itinerant contacts in offices in southern Canada, and in snowhouses, tents and ships' cabins in Arctic Canada, of the following individuals: Dr. R. Thorsteinsson, Dr. T. Tozer, and Dr. Y. O. Fortier, of the Geological Survey of Canada – on geology and minerals; Dr. F. Mueller of the Dept. of Geography, McGill University, Dr. G. Hattersley-Smith of the Defence Research Board, Dr. Vilhjalmur Stefansson (deceased), Commodore O. C. S. Robertson (ret.) R. C. N. and Miss Moira Dunbar of the Defence Research Board – on ice; Dr. M. J. Dunbar, Fisheries Research Board – on the subject of the sea; Singeetuk (deceased) of Rankin Inlet, Idlouk (deceased) of Resolute Bay, Itteemangnak of Pelly Bay and Attungala of Baker Lake, Dr. J. S. Tener, C. R. Harington, J. P. Kelsall and A. Loughery of the Canadian Wildlife Service – on animals; Dr. D. B. O. Saville, Dept of Agriculture, Dr. A. E. Porsild (ret.), National Museum of Canada, Kidlak (deceased) of Pond Inlet – plants; Dr. D. R. Oliver, Dept. of Agriculture – on insects; Dr. W. E. Taylor, Jr., National Museum of Canada, Graham Rowley, Dept. of Indian Affairs and Northern Development, Akomalik (deceased) of Pond Inlet – on Eskimo history; Alex. Stevenson, Dept. of Indian Affairs and Northern Development, Patrick Baird, McGill University, Henry Larsen (deceased), R. C. M. P., P. E. C. Nichols, Hudson's Bay Company, Father F. van de Velde, O.M.I., Oblate Missions and Canon J. James, Anglican Missions, on the Arctic.

PICTURE CREDITS

Order of appearance in the text of pictures listed here is left to right, top to bottom.

Cover/National Film Board
1/Fred Bruemmer
2-21/Doug Wilkinson
22/National Air Photo Library
23/National Film Board
24-31/Doug Wilkinson
40/John de Visser
45-53/Doug Wilkinson
57-71/Fred Bruemmer
72/John de Visser, Dr. G. Peck, Dr. Donald R. Gunn
73/Dr. G. Peck, Fred Bruemmer, Dr. R. R. Tasker, Barry Ranford
74/Dr. D. R. Gunn, Dr. G. Peck, Dr. D. R. Gunn
75/Fred Bruemmer
79/Ernest Kuyt
93-97/Dr. G. Peck
98/Fred Bruemmer, Dr. G. Peck
99/Dr. G. Peck, Barry Ranford, Dr. G. Peck, Dr. G. Peck
100-107/Fred Bruemmer
108/Fred Bruemmer, S. D. MacDonald, Fred Bruemmer, Fred Bruemmer, Fred Bruemmer
109/E. Kuyt, John de Visser, National Film Board
110-113/Fred Bruemmer
119/John de Visser
120/Doug Wilkinson, John de Visser, John de Visser, National Film Board
121/John de Visser
122/Fred Bruemmer
125/John de Visser
128/Dr. G. Peck
132/Glenbow Archives Calgary
133/Geological Survey of Canada
134/National Film Board
137-140/Toronto Public Libraries
141/Doug Wilkinson

This book was produced entirely in Canada by:
Mono Lino Typesetting Co. Limited / *Typesetting;* Herzig Somerville Limited / *Film Separation;*
Ashton-Potter Limited / *Printing;* T. H. Best Printing Co. Limited / *Binding.*
Typefaces: Times New Roman and Helvetica. Paper: 65 lb. Georgian Offset Smooth.
PRINTED IN CANADA

G H I J K 79 78 77 76 75 74